THE PLAN THAT LAUNCHED a**THOUSAND BOOKS**

by Tara R. Alemany

Books published by Emerald Lake Books may be ordered through booksellers or by contacting:

Emerald Lake Books
44 Green Pond Rd
Sherman, CT 06784

http://emeraldlakebooks.com
860-946-0544

Rev. Date: 10/07/2014

ISBN: 978-0692308752

I have two bestsellers under my belt and I wish I had read this book before I had written them. This would have saved me a lot of time and money. A big help to a new author!

Jeffrey Hayzlett,
Primetime TV Show Host,
Bestselling Author and Sometime Cowboy

Tara's book offers great tips from page one. If you are thinking of publishing your own book, find out what you need to know from Tara Alemany. Highly recommended!

Chris Westfall,
National Elevator Pitch Champion
and Author of *BulletProof Branding*

Books by Tara R. Alemany

The Plan that Launched a Thousand Books

The Character-Based Leader

My Love to You Always

Celebrating 365 Days of Gratitude (2013 ed.)

The Best is Yet to Come

*This book is dedicated to
anyone who has ever had a burning desire
to see their own words
between the covers of a book
and pursued that dream,
and to the many hundreds of my
audience members, readers and clients
who have sought my guidance
in making their dreams a reality.*

DOWNLOAD THE PRINTABLE PREPARING TO MARKET YOUR BOOK TEMPLATE

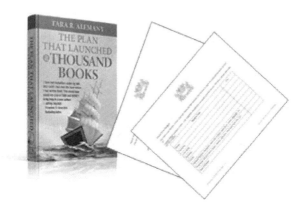

Read This First

Just to say "thank you" for purchasing
The Plan that Launched a Thousand Books,
I'd like to give you a free template to help you
get started with your book marketing plan.

Just go to alewebsocial.com/ThePlanTemplate
to download the template as my gift to you.

Contents

Preface

The publishing world has changed significantly in the recent past. Publishers have become much more selective about which books they choose to publish, and often they require that the writer be established already somehow.

This leaves new writers with little choice but to go with a smaller, less selective, publishing house or to self-publish, both respectable options. If self-publishing worked for the likes of Mark Twain, John Grisham, L. Ron Hubbard, Walt Whitman, Richard Paul Evans, Jack Canfield and Mark Victor Hansen, Beatrix Potter, Edgar Allan Poe, T.S. Elliot, e.e. cummings, Tom Clancy, E. L. James and many others, it can certainly work for you too!

Yet given the circumstances, small publishers and self-publishing options cannot provide the same solutions or services that a larger publishing house is able to. Much of the hard work of selling your book falls to you. But who is better suited to do it? You *know* your book.

Marketing, publicity, events coordination, book tours, distribution and more, which used to be the responsibility of the publisher, now often falls to the writer. For some writers, this can be overwhelming, because they don't even know where to start. What's the inevitable result? Most self-published authors typically sell fewer than 175 copies of their books. Just to put that in context, 78% of all titles released during 2011 were released from a small press or self-publisher.

So, a lot of new titles just aren't gaining the traction that they could, and this is a direct result of the fact that many of the things traditionally handled by the publisher are now being left for the author to do themselves, and they haven't a clue where to begin.

In addition to the marketing and publicity issues, there are decisions that need to be made regarding which formats to publish a book in as well. Print or digital? For print copies, which trim size, paper color, and binding would be best? If a digital format is chosen, which eBook formats will be supported? They're not all alike! And will you be creating auxiliaries to the book, like audiobooks, workbooks and other related materials? If so, how will they be distributed? Bundled with the book or as separate items?

There is typically only a slight additional cost to publishing in eBook format. As a result, 85% of eBooks produced are created *in addition* to printed books. Okay, but which format? Well... 60% of eBook sales actually take place on Amazon. That means that the remaining 40% are sold across all of the other online retailer sites, like the Barnes and Noble website, iBookstore, Kobo and more, which might help you make an informed decision as to where you want to spend your money, at least for now.

Many self-publishing firms offer an eBook option as part of a bundled package. So long as the Amazon Kindle format is part of the mix, go for it! However, don't be too quick to dismiss the need for the other formats. The eBook sales and distribution market is growing rapidly, and other EPUB-based platforms and channels are gaining traction. That does not mean that sales are down at Amazon though. It's simply that the market is growing and Amazon's sales margin isn't growing at the same rapid pace as the rest of the industry.

With all of these different decisions to make, it's no wonder that authors who are left to handle all of this on their own have no idea how to proceed or what to do next. They didn't sign on to be a publisher. They followed their dream of being a writer. And there's a *big* difference! But that's what this plan is going to help you with.

It'll give you a starting place to work from and, hopefully, you'll find that you don't need to be another statistic with only 175 copies of your book sold.

This is when commitment to your book needs to take over. The writing is done. It's time to get it into the hands of your readers now.

Jack Canfield, co-author of the Chicken Soup for the Soul series, skyrocketed to fame because he made a commitment to himself to do five things to promote the first book every single day. He calls this "The Rule of 5." This could mean signing five books and giving them to people for free. It could be giving talks at churches or sending out free copies to reviewers or giving five radio interviews. There were five specific actions he and his partner, Mark Victor Hansen, did every day so there was always something happening that promoted the book.

You're getting ready to start on the same journey. Congratulations on purchasing this plan to help you get started! It's a great first step.

But the reality is, unless you're committed to doing something every day to promote your book, it's never going to sell the way you'd like it too. This is not a one-shot solution where you do the things in this book once and you're all set. You have to incorporate the recommendations in this plan into your existing marketing plan. If you don't have one, use this as the basis of the one you're going to create.

So, are you committed to your success? If not, close this book, file it away somewhere, and try to remember to come back to it later when you're finally ready. But if you're ready now, let's get started!

Getting Started

To market your book effectively online, you are going to do three things; define your target audience, create a content-rich online presence, and build relationships through social networks and in-person networking. These marketing activities will help you to stand out in an increasingly noisy world, generating more exposure for your book.

As you establish yourself as a genuine and insightful person who has interesting things to share, the people you are connected to will naturally gravitate towards buying your product (and recommending it to their friends too).

Sounds simple, right? Well... Yes and no. There are only three things we need to do, but there are an unlimited number of ways to do them. This plan is going to cover just 25 different ways to promote your book that will get your book marketing off to a great start. And here they are:

1. Begin outlining your book marketing plan.
2. Work with your publisher to determine what promotional services they offer and take advantage of them.
3. Include an advertisement in the back of your book or see if an affiliate is willing to do so.
4. Create or update your website.
5. Blog about your book.
6. Find others willing to blog about your book.
7. Launch a reviewer outreach campaign.
8. Consider using affiliates to market your book.
9. Seek out guest spots on relevant podcasts, livecasts, teleseminars and webinars.
10. Optimize your presence on Amazon.com.

11. Optimize your presence on BarnesandNoble.com.

12. Distribute your book in eBook format.

13. Give your reader other choices.

14. Establish yourself on Facebook.

15. Provide engaging content on Pinterest.

16. Participate on Twitter.

17. Create a YouTube channel.

18. Leverage LinkedIn.

19. Use the best features of Google+.

20. Mobilize your network.

21. Offer free samples related to your book in eBook format.

22. Get listed.

23. Submit your book to award competitions.

24. Participate in and promote events.

25. Launch a bestseller campaign.

26. Establish a joint venture (JV) partner program.

27. Attend networking meetings with books in hand.

28. Create innovative book signing events.

29. Create press releases.

30. Update your e-mail signature.

31. Find non-bookstore buyers.

32. Launch a crowdsourcing campaign.

Alright... I know that's more than 25 things. But it's an example of how you need to market your book. *Always* over-deliver in anything you do. When you do this authentically, people take notice. When you do this consistently, you increase your sales.

Anyway, don't feel like this is a comprehensive list or that these are the only things you can do. And don't believe that you have to do every one of these things. However, this is where I typically start with my clients when I help them promote their new books, and you can get started with the same approach too.

Pick and choose those things that you want to do and are able to, and then outsource or skip those that you aren't comfortable doing.

Some things, like developing a Facebook presence, may be better left to an expert to do. While anyone can create a Facebook page, it does take a specialized knowledge to create a robust page where all of your books are listed and available for sale with an effective landing page and what's called a "lead capture" box, where people can sign up for your mailing list.

You may also find that you want to outsource those activities that are on-going, and therefore may become time-consuming. When the budget allows, that's always a nice thing to do. But oftentimes, first-time writers have to take on as much of everything as they can to keep costs down. You've come to the right place. This plan will definitely lay the groundwork for you to get started!

As you read through this book, you will find links to recommended resources throughout it. At the time of this writing, all of the links were working links, but given the changing nature of the internet, some may change over time. I've also found in the 2 years since I released the first edition of this book that many of the tools and services that I use with my clients are changing.

As a result, I've have created a Resources page on my website, specifically for readers of *The Plan*. Simply go to alewebsocial.com/ThePlanResources to get a current list of recommended tools and resources.

The first few topics in the plan may be obvious, like building your book's brand on various social networking sites. But there are a lot of other things you can (and should) be doing to promote your book too. When it comes right down to it, if you can think of a place where you *might* be found online, you should be there. Many options are free or low-cost, but they all involve work.

So, are you ready? Let's start first with understanding who it is that you're trying to reach and how you plan to reach them.

Developing Your Own Unique Plan

There are a number of elements that go into developing a marketing plan for your specific book. It starts first with understanding the mission of the book.

Was the book written in order to give you more visibility as an expert in your field? Or is it part of a passion project, something that means a lot to you and that you want to support? Is it an extension of your business brand or a standalone product? Will you use it to generate new clients or are you simply looking for readers? Is it an installment in a series or is it complete on its own?

Think about why you're launching the book. Why does it exist?

The mission of your book should be something that you can share in one sentence. Make it tweetable! See if you can keep it 140 characters or less.

Developing a marketing plan for your book is one of the most important tasks you need to complete in order to promote your book successfully. However it starts with understanding your *Why*. Why was it written and what will it accomplish? Whose lives will be impacted by it? What will be the outcome of that impact?

Once you've established that information, the rest will fall into place more easily. Otherwise, you're using a scattershot approach and praying that it hits somebody. That's not a very effective use of your time or resources.

As you work on your marketing plan, there are other questions to consider as well. What are your book marketing goals? Identify some measurable targets so that you can see the progress that you are making.

Know who your ideal reader is. Develop a clear picture in your mind. Your book will not appeal to everyone and that's okay. Create a prototype of your ideal reader by considering age, gender, marital status, interests and other demographics. This will help you to pinpoint the right strategies for reaching them.

Of course we all think that our book will appeal to everyone. The problem is, you can't market to everyone at once. There's just not enough impact. To successfully market your book, you want to define a target reader for each campaign that you run.

In addition to knowing your reader, be sure to do some research and understand what the competing titles are for your book. There are two primary reasons to spend time on this. First, the author of the competing title with a similar audience may be a prime endorsement candidate for your book. Second, you can look at how those other titles are being marketed and learn from what's working and avoid what's not.

One particular tool that I like to use for this purpose is a Google Chrome extension called KindleSpy.[1] It allows you to go to an Amazon author page or a category listing and pull key information about the Kindle eBooks listed there. For each of the books shown, KindleSpy tells you its price, estimated number of sales and resulting revenue, the number of reviews, and its overall sales rank, as well as the average price and revenue, sales rank and number of reviews. It will also show you a word cloud based on the bestselling books in the category, as well as the top 5 words used in their titles.

If you want to see it in action, you can check out my review and the video demo I recorded in "Researching Killer Topics Using KindleSpy"[2] and read about further tips on using KindleSpy in "Find Bestselling Book Ideas Using KindleSpy."[3]

---

[1] alewebsocial.com/KindleSpy
[2] alewebsocial.com/KindleSpyDemo
[3] alewebsocial.com/KindleSpyLI

Using a tool like this allows you to research your competition easily, so you can see which books are selling the best. But it also allows you to research and prioritize your own projects, and come up with book titles that are sure to appeal to today's potential readers.

Having a clear understanding of what the competing titles are also allows you to identify how your book is different than theirs. Leverage what makes you unique.

The nice thing is, you can export the data as well so that you can look at it in more detail, take your time with it, sort the information the way you want, and develop your strategies from there.

In these early planning stages, consider who you might ask to endorse your book. Yes there are authors of competing titles, but perhaps there are other celebrities who might be suitable too.

Ideally you want to be thinking about potential endorsers even before you've gotten too deep into the writing. If you're writing a business book, being able to cite case studies and examples that favorably showcase a prospective endorser's favorite company or nonprofit can go a long way to securing their endorsement.

And if you're an unknown author, sometimes the biggest selling point can be a celebrity endorsement on your cover. If you've never heard of me before, perhaps the endorsement of a 2-time NYT bestselling author like Jeffrey Hayzlett on my cover made you feel a bit more comfortable about spending a little money on what I had to share, right?

At least that's the theory. His endorsement doesn't make my material any more valid than it was without it, but it reduces the perceived risk of following my advice when someone who has already accomplished what you want to achieve says "Take a look!"

Once you've considered all of these factors and come up with a solid marketing plan that includes clear actions and measurable goals, then it's time to get started on the real work! If you need a template to help you put it all together, I have one you can request for free at alewebsocial.com/ThePlanTemplate. (It's the same one as was mentioned at the beginning of the book.)

Publisher Promotions

If you've used a small publishing house, you'll find that many publishers have a blog on their website, where they encourage their authors to submit content related to their book. If that option is available to you, seize it! If it's not, be sure to ask the publisher you're dealing with what, if any, support they give for promoting your book. For example, they may not have a blog, but perhaps they're willing to help promote your online efforts via their Facebook page or newsletter. Until you ask, you won't know what the options are. So, don't wait!

They have a vested interest, more often than not, in seeing you succeed. It's great for their brand awareness if one of the books they published makes it on a bestseller list somewhere or is recognized in other interesting ways.

If you find that they don't offer any outlets for you to promote your book through them, you may want to take a moment to educate them on the benefits. When you succeed, they get to ride your coat-tails since other potential authors see their name on your book and equate it with success.

Unfortunately, what you'll most likely find is that they offer marketing packages to you at an additional cost. This is where developing an understanding of the publishing industry will come in handy.

For example, many vanity publishers will offer you the opportunity to purchase a plan that allows bookstores to return unused quantities of your book. This is vital because a bookstore doesn't want to get stuck with unsold copies of any book, so once it's been on the shelf awhile, if it hasn't sold, they want the option to return the unsold quantities to the publisher.

Sounds reasonable, right? Well... Yes and no. You see, unless you've already proven yourself as a marketer and have strong sales figures and notoriety to go along with your book's appeal, they're not likely to put your book on the shelf in the first place! So, why spend money on something that's not likely to be used?

In-book Advertising

If you've written other books, but they're unrelated, list them on a page called "Other Books by {You}." When a reader finds someone that they enjoy reading, they will often look for other titles by the same author, whether the books are related or not.

Alternatively, you could include the first chapter of the next book at the end of the one they've just finished reading. This gives them the chance to sample it and hopefully get sucked in to it. This works particularly well if the books are related in some way (part of a series or in a similar genre).

By extension if your book is an installment in a series, make sure that you let the reader know that other titles exist in the series. Sometimes, my clients include an advertising page at the back of the book that announces the other titles in the series or introduces auxiliary materials, like a related workbook or audiobook. This works especially well for non-fiction, business-related books, but I've seen it used in a variety of genres.

Website

Once you've found out what the marketing options are through your publisher and your book is all set, the next place to focus on is your website.

Ideally, you want to have a website long before the book launch, simply so that it gains some traction early. This becomes a ready platform for you to build anticipation about the impending release of your book, as well as to keep people apprised of book-related activities, like book signings, etc. You'll be using this lead time to create strong relationships with potential readers who anticipate the release of your book. Get them excited about what's yet to come.

The first step in setting up your website is to register the domain name. A domain name is your web address. I have a few. My business domain is alewebsocial.com. However, I also have emeraldlakebooks.com for my publishing imprint, tararalemany.com for my speaking and writing, bitesizedmarketer.com for my video tutorial service, and inspiringhopein.us for an inspirational conference that I host each year.

When you select a domain name, you want to choose carefully. It should relate either to your book title, the subject of your book, your name (if you plan to have an author site with separate pages for each of your titles), your brand, or the overarching message or theme of your writing.

And don't hesitate to use some of the new domain extensions that are out there. Yes, we're all familiar with the .coms, but sometimes a different domain extension makes perfect sense, like when I selected inspiringhopein.us. I loved how the completed domain when read aloud echoed the message of the conference, "Inspiring Hope in Us."

Whatever you choose should be easy to spell and remember. If you have one of those last names that consist of random consonants and too few vowels, you may want to skip using it in favor of something your audience is more likely to be able to spell.

You can use Namechk (namechk.com) to verify the availability of the domain name you'd like to use in addition to all the relevant social profiles you may want to claim.

After you settle on a domain name, register it with a domain name service like GoDaddy[4] or HostGator.[5] I

---

[4] godaddy.com

typically use GoDaddy to register domain names and HostGator to serve as my web host. Even though both companies offer registration and hosting services, I have found that this set-up works best for me.)

Once you have your domain selected and registered, you want to make sure that you've got a great description on your website regarding your book. It should be clear to the reader right away whether your book is fiction or non-fiction, and whether it is already released or soon to be published. Add your book's cover image as well to let your readers start becoming familiar with it. As you start gathering reviews of your book, repost them here so that potential readers can see what others are saying about it. Alternatively, you can create what some people call a "carnival post," where you include a short segment of multiple recent reviews with links back to the full review elsewhere.

---

[5] alewebsocial.com/HostGator. Use the coupon code "AlewebAuthors" to receive a 25% discount on a new account.

If you don't have a website or your website doesn't support blogging, I strongly recommend that you get yourself a simple Wordpress site. If you use Wordpress.com to create your site, you'll be able to include a page for your book, as well as pages for your speaking schedule, your blog, your bio, etc. However, you will only be able to include links to another eCommerce site (like Amazon or your publisher's site) to sell your book. You won't be able to sell books directly on your Wordpress.com site.

When you channel your sales through another site, you do lose the cut that they take in exchange for distributing your books for you. So, weigh out the pros and cons of sending traffic away from your website to Amazon or elsewhere rather than selling the books on your site, and handling the packaging and shipping yourself. The latter option is more work, but enables you to keep more of the proceeds and have greater control over the price of your book. The former option ensures greater visibility and the potential to reach bestseller status, and ensures that the sales are tracked against your ISBN (a unique identifier for your book), which is important if you hope to secure a contract with a traditional publisher later on.

You may find that the best answer for you is to do both, using the Amazon presence early on to achieve bestseller status, and then shifting to driving sales from your website later on when the demand isn't as great!

If you decide that you want to be able to sell your books directly on your site, it means that you'll have to create what's called a "self-hosted" Wordpress site instead. You do that by going to Wordpress.org (not .com) and following the instructions there. You'll also need to register with a web host (to "self-host" your website). I recommend HostGator because it is easy to use, the price is reasonable, and the tech support is great.

While it can be intimidating for some, the instructions are clear and easy to follow. So, don't psych yourself out.

Give it a try! You can always change your mind later and hire someone to finish it for you.

When asked for my opinion about whether to start with Wordpress.com or a self-hosted Wordpress site, I always recommend the self-hosted version. While it may take more effort to set up to begin with, it can grow with you. As you build your audience and want to increase your offerings, a Wordpress.com site will eventually be unable to keep up with what you will want and need to do. Then you'll have the added expense of migrating your existing content to a self-hosted site, rather than simply starting there to begin with.

The biggest step in building a website, whether you use Wordpress.com or a self-hosted Wordpress site, is to select the theme that you're going to base your site on. Themes for Wordpress.com are contained within the Wordpress.com site. So, you can review what's available once you begin creating your site. Themes for self-hosted sites are available all over the internet. Do a Google search on "Wordpress themes," and see what comes up. If you want to stick with those themes that are free, search on "free Wordpress themes" instead.

Some of the more popular self-hosted Wordpress themes are made by Studio Press,[6] the creators of the Genesis framework, which has hundreds of child themes available. If you don't know where to start, and want as much control over the look and feel of a site as possible, without having to know a lot of CSS (code that allows you to customize your site), I recommend starting with the Prose theme for Genesis. Its design settings allow you to easily adjust colors, font sizes, link decorations, etc. with minimal effort.

Plugins designed to work specifically with Genesis and Prose extend the functionality even more, allowing you to add more features, footers and widgets as needed.

---

[6] alewebsocial.com/Genesis

Make sure as you select your theme that you take into consideration the overall layout you want your website to have. By default, you'll get a blog page. That's good. But do you want a sidebar? (Actually, yes, you do, since you'll want to include an e-mail sign-up form so that you can build your mailing list.) Do you want the sidebar on the left or right? (I recommend the right, since it's friendlier for mobile devices.) One sidebar? Two? Or more? Perhaps you want a different layout all together or to have a portfolio of books?

As you make these decisions, you can refine your search terms further to narrow down the options a bit more.

Try to find a theme that comes as close as possible to what you want, recognizing that you can swap out the images and text, but the size and placement should be just about perfect. The closer the theme comes to what you want, the less likely it is that you'll have to get a developer involved to "fix" your site the way you want it.

Another consideration in selecting a theme is whether they are "mobile-friendly." Industry experts predict that by 2015, there will be more internet activity using mobile devices than laptops! Given the surge in smartphones, iPads and other such devices, the Mobile Age is here. There's no sense creating a site today that's going to be seriously out-dated next year. So, look for a theme that supports mobile access as well as the other features you're interested in having.

Once you've settled on the technical aspects of your website, it's time to populate it with great content. In addition to a description of your book, consider adding excerpts from it to give readers a sense of the storyline or even recording an audio excerpt that they can listen to. If they like what they see, they'll want to buy it. So, make it easy for them to do so.

While you may be selling your book on Amazon, Barnes & Noble and other online retailers, don't forget that you can sell it on your own website too.

Use a simple shopping cart plugin, like Ecwid,[7] to list your products on your site. The thing I like most about Ecwid is that it's a fully functioning storefront that can handle taxable and non-taxable items. For things like eBooks, automatic downloads can be set up so that once the payment is processed, the purchaser is immediately sent their product. For physical products, you can authorize Ecwid to gather actual shipping costs for each order placed so that you never have to calculate any of that information for your products. You provide the weight in the product description, the purchaser provides their zip code, and Ecwid does the rest.

And to make things even better, you can define the store once and use it both on your website and on Facebook. No duplication of effort there, and you get to keep 100% of the proceeds.

---

[7] alewebsocial.com/Ecwid

The only flaw I currently see regarding Ecwid is that you can specify the product price and weight, but not a handling charge. Shipping costs are calculated based on the product weight and the shipping method the buyer selects. Since there's no separate location to add a handling charge, you either need to roll that into your product price or expense it. According to the Ecwid developer forum though, this is something they intend to address in the future.

Another limitation to be aware of is that the free version of Ecwid only allows you to add up to 10 products unless you have a grandfathered account. If you want to list more, then you need to upgrade to the premium version.

Moving on, another thing to consider is adding a page to your website with a list of all the different places that your book is available for them to purchase. While you'll probably make the most profit on those copies you sell yourself, you also want to make it easy for the person to buy. Knowing that they can go down to their local Barnes & Noble and pick up a copy of your book as a last-minute birthday gift for Aunt Sally could be the difference between making that sale or losing it. So, don't be afraid to tell them where else they can purchase copies of your book.

Personally, I like using a plugin called "MyBooks for Authors" by Out:think Group.[8] It creates beautifully formatted listings for each of your books, along with recognizable buy links to the various online retailers where your book is sold. Unfortunately, as of October 2014, it appears this plugin is no longer available and inquiries to the developer have gone unanswered, so you'll have to do a little research to find an alternative.

Always make sure that your website contains information about you, who you are as a writer and as a person. This creates a sense of familiarity and connection

---

[8] alewebsocial.com/Outthink

with prospective readers who will look forward to getting to know you better.

Offer a reason for visitors to subscribe to your mailing list, whether it's a free download, a sample chapter or a short call with you. I recommend using MailChimp[9] when you're first getting started because it's free until you have 2,000 people on your mailing list. So, use that time as you're growing your list to become familiar with how e-mail marketing works and develop your strategies for how you want to use it to stay connected to your readers.

Another way to increase engagement on your site is to include what's called an "active responder" on the site. I don't recommend those pop-ups that appear when someone first enters your site, because if they're new there, they haven't had a chance to even experience your content yet to decide if they want to join. So, it creates a

---

[9] alewebsocial.com/MailChimp

negative state-of-mind before the visitor has even started to get to know you.

By the same token, I don't recommend the pop-ups that are displayed when someone tries to navigate away from your site. It's another guerilla tactic that creates a negative, high-pressure experience.

Instead, what I recommend and use on my sites is an active engagement plugin called "vCita." [10] This pop-up appears discreetly after the visitor has had a chance to experience your site for a bit. (You configure how long.) It allows the visitor to send you a message or schedule an appointment. That's a completely different thing than plugging joining your mailing list, because it offers a two-way connection. That's much more appealing than being marketed to, and is often accepted by the reader who is excited for an opportunity to connect with you.

---

[10] alewebsocial.com/vCita

I also recommended using a backup plugin that runs on an automated schedule so that your site is being regularly backed up in the event of a crash or technical error. My favorite plugin for this is called "BackupBuddy" by iThemes,[11] but there are a number of them out there that each have slightly different features. So, find the one that's right for you and your website needs.

Once you start getting traffic to your website, make sure that you've put analytics in place (like Google Analytics[12]) so that you can track where visitors are coming from, and what content they seem to like the most.

You'll also want to install a Site Map plugin so that Google can easily tell what's on your site. I recommend either the Simple Google Sitemap XML plugin by iTx Technologies[13] or Wordpress SEO by Yoast,[14] which

---

[11] alewebsocial.com/BackupBuddy
[12] google.com/analytics
[13] alewebsocial.com/SimpleSitemap

creates a sitemap for you, but does not submit it like Simple Google Sitemap does. So if you rely upon the Yoast plugin, you'll have to go into Google's Webmaster Tools[15] and submit the sitemaps yourself.

Submitting your website to the search engines by registering the site map will increase your website's visibility and ultimately your book sales.

As you think through what you want your website to accomplish for you, consider the points Jane Friedman makes in her article "Build a More Effective Author Website." [16] In it, she outlines elements you definitely want to have on your site and common mistakes that she sees on author websites. I run into the same mistakes all of the time on author websites, especially the one about whether the site is mobile friendly or not. As I said before, these days, the majority of internet access is done from

---

[14] alewebsocial.com/SEObyYoast

[15] google.com/webmasters

[16] alewebsocial.com/FriedmanArticle

smartphones and tablets. So, make sure that your content is going to be accessible no matter what the device being used is!

Keywords

As you create additional content for your website, keep in mind that search engines rank sites according to their relevance. Your web page content will only be relevant if it relates to you and your book.

Search engines find keywords in two primary areas, within the content of your website and within special fields in the code of your website called "metadata." Just to be clear, *keywords* are the words people type in when they use search engines. Therefore, it's important that the keywords for your site match the terms people use to look for you. It's the only way that the search engine can match your content to the information people are looking for.

If you're using a Wordpress site, you'll want to add an SEO (search engine optimization) plugin to the site so that you have control over the metadata for each page and post of your site. While I used to recommend that my clients use the All in One SEO Pack by Michael Torbert,[17] I'm leaning more toward using the Wordpress SEO by Yoast plugin mentioned earlier. It's a more robust tool that replaces multiple plugins that I used to use. Either one will work well though. Both are excellent tools.

When you talk about SEO for a website, many people recommend using keyword tools like Google's Keyword Analyzer[18] to find which keywords people are searching for. While that will tell you what search terms people are using, it won't tell you what's on your own site. Therefore, when I'm working with my clients to establish optimize existing content on their site, I'm much more likely to use a tool like Wordle.net than I am to use the Keyword Analyzer.

---

[17] alewebsocial.com/AllinOneSEO
[18] alewebsocial.com/GoogleKeyword

I'll recommend the Keyword Analyzer if the content isn't written yet and we want to get a clear picture of what terms are more likely to be popular. But not for figuring out whether we've targeted the right keywords for the site. When we do use the Keyword Analyzer in preparation of writing new content, we select both high and low competition keywords to include in the text.

Wordle analyzes web content and gives you a word cloud representation of the most commonly used terms. *Those* are the terms you want to be using as the focus keyword in the SEO plugin for the page you've analyzed. You can add any other terms that you like to the keywords, just make sure they exist on the page you're adding them to.

Blogging

Blogging is a powerful source of visibility for many reasons. First, it's fresh content, which the search engines like to see. Second, it's easy for readers to share with their friends. Third, it brings traffic to your website, increasing its visibility to the search engines. Fourth, it's more information on the internet that's all about *your book*!

When it comes to blogging, you should maintain your own, seek out opportunities to guest blog on other people's sites, and give people reasons to blog about you and your book.

There are many ways to find blogs to guest post on. Some take more time than others. Typically, you want to find blogs you like and enjoy following, build a relationship with that blog's owner, and see if they ever use guest bloggers on their site. However, there are shortcuts you can take. For instance, on Triberr,[19] you can see all of the bloggers who are posting book reviews. Spend some time looking at what they are reviewing, and identifying bloggers who may be right for your particular book.

---

[19] alewebsocial.com/Triberr

I also use BloggerLinkUp to connect with people who are looking for guest posts, as well as those who are offering them. [20]

You should also ask any reviewers that blog about your book to post their review in your online book listing (on Amazon, Barnes and Noble, Goodreads or wherever else you want people to go to learn about and buy your book). And make sure that when someone takes the time to review your book on their blog, you promote their post to your network, share it on your website, and publicly thank them for their comments (even if it's only as a comment on their blog).

Pay particular attention to their blog post too and be sure to make yourself available to respond to reader comments.

---

[20] alewebsocial.com/BloggerLinkUp

Blogging (Your Own)

Once your website is ready, it's time to start using it! So, how do you get started? Well, you can start building interest in your book by blogging about favorite passages, the writing process, the experiences you're encountering promoting the book, etc. Consider sharing some of the "inner workings" of an author's journey, and any book-centric topics that will inspire people to read it. If you already have a following, poll people for their top choice of cover design. Bring them into the process, and allow them to feel a sense of connectedness to what's going on.

If you were offering the book to your best friend and it wasn't yours, how would you describe it? What would you want to share with them? Consider those things, and then write about them!

As you write blog posts, make sure that you let people know they're there. Post links in appropriate groups, social networks, and in your e-mail newsletter. Ask people you know to share the information with their friends as well, and to subscribe to your blog. You can add social sharing buttons to any page on your website, including individual blog posts. There are plenty of social sharing plugins available for Wordpress sites. Two popular ones are ShareThis and SexyBookmarks by Shareaholic.

Alternatively, you can add your own code to the site instead of using an existing plugin. The Facebook Like button, the TweetMeme Retweet button, the LinkedIn Share button, and the Pinterest Pin It button are just a few of the many options out there. Follow the instructions provided for implementing them on your own site.

Blogging on your own website keeps the content fresh, which keeps the search engines (and interested readers) coming back for more. Ideally, you want to be posting at least 2 times a week on your blog, with pieces that are as few as 250 words or as many as 1200. Just make sure that, for longer pieces, you break up the content with headings, bullets and images to make it easy to read.

The more content you generate, the more visits you attract. So, posting regularly can have an effect on how favorably the search engines react to your site.

Additionally, knowing your target audience is critical in determining an appropriate post length and format. Each generation has a different method of processing information. In general, Baby Boomers enjoy reading, so a longer, text-based post is fine with them. However, the Millennials (those born between 1982 and 2004) prefer shorter, more interactive posts, including video content. Generations even younger than that want to control the information they receive, so polls, games, contests, etc. are more enticing to them.

Regardless of the post length, frequency and format, make certain that the content is engaging enough to keep your ideal audience reading. They don't want to be bombarded with irrelevant or unappealing information.

Start by asking a question or presenting a problem that catches the reader's attention. Then answer that question for them. Readers often find it easiest to follow along if you employ lists in the data, but that's a stylistic issue related to how you convey your content, and I leave that decision up to you.

As you are writing though, make sure that you are incorporating the high and low competition keywords you've identified using Google's Keyword Analyzer into your post. This will optimize it so that it has a greater chance of appearing on page one of Google.

I also recommend using video blogs (or "vlogs") periodically. This is where your blog post consists primarily of a short, 30-90 second video. Start with a brief description of the video, followed by the video content itself. This gives your readers a chance to get to know you, and often takes less time to put together than a written post.

However, if you opt to create a vlog post, the search engines can't see that content. So, I still recommend transcribing the audio and posting that in the body of the post as well or, at the very least, summarize the content below the video to give the search engines something to work with. If you're short on resources and want to include the transcript, I recommend using Speechpad.com to my clients. This transcription service creates human-generated transcripts in short turnaround times for reasonable prices.

End every post with some kind of "call to action." In other words, let the reader know what it is that you'd like them to do as a result of what they've read. It can be something as simple as "Share your thoughts in the Comments below" or "Check back later this week for our next topic" or "If you found this interesting, you'll want to read... too." You can also invite them to join your mailing list, share the post, or whatever else seems right and appropriate at the time. But only give the reader one action to follow. If you give too many options, they're likely to choose none.

Always make sure that you respond to comments that your readers leave for you, ideally within 24 hours. This outward sign that you are invested in your website and interested in engaging with them keeps them coming back for more.

For those that want additional help with this crucial part of marketing your book, I'd recommend purchasing Copyblogger Media's "31 Days to Build a Better Blog." [21] It's written in a workbook format that's available in an instant download. Its author, Darren Rowe, walks you through step-by-step with a new task each day that explains both the *how* and the *why* of the task, and offering further reading resources if you want to dig deeper into a specific topic.

---

[21] alewebsocial.com/31Days

Blogging (Others)

One of the easiest ways to build the buzz about a product is to get other people writing about it. I describe it as being "easy" because it's hard to come up with things to say about our own work at times. (There's a natural resistance to it.) But I say it also because you can leverage the time and talents of a group of people all writing about your book, instead of doing it all yourself.

A typical way of achieving this is to reach out to a limited portion of your community and find those who might be interested in receiving a pre-release or review copy of your book in exchange for helping you "build the buzz" about it. You'll find many people that will take you up on the offer, and most will write a post about you or ask you for an interview for their readers. Then, you can cross-promote the post so that your following is visiting their website as well as their following visiting yours.

You may also want to reserve a few review copies for strategically selected reviewers that you approach. You can search for influential bloggers related to your topic and ask them privately whether they'd be interested in reviewing your book. Be sure to put your request in context though. Don't simply ask them for something (a review). Let them know what stood out about them, their blog, or their audience that makes them seem like a good fit. And be clear about what it is that you'd like them to do. For example, ask them if they'd add their review comments to your Amazon book listing or give you a testimonial for your website. Since they can link their review back to their own site, which is a potential source of website traffic for them, they should be willing.

Be strategic in your thinking as you select these influential people. If they are already famous, everyone is probably asking for their help, so it will be hard for you to stand out from the crowd. Unless you already know someone famous, you may want to select someone who has a solid, large following that makes them influential, but may not necessarily be famous yet. I often will use Wefollow.com, a Twitter directory that people opt into and add themselves to the categories they feel they represent. Find a category relevant to your book and start building connections with the approachable leaders of that category.

There are a number of ways to identify influential bloggers. You may want to use a combination of checking Klout[22] or Kred[23] scores of people already identified as being influential about the subject of your book. Then, also use Google's blogsearch function[24] to identify blogs related to your topic. Additionally, use Alexa.com to search for websites relevant to your book. The nice thing about using Alexa to do this search is that you can see within the results themselves how heavily trafficked those websites are. The more traffic a site gets, the more visibility for your book. Trusting that you get a great review, that's a wonderful thing!

---

[22] alewebsocial.com/Klout
[23] alewebsocial.com/Kred
[24] google.com/blogsearch

Alternatively, you can select a handful of bloggers that you'd really like to have read your book and simply send them a signed copy, stating that you hope they enjoy it. Will every one of them read and review it? No. But some of them will. These individuals should be strategically selected though, and should be people you respect and admire. This is not an approach to take with just anyone.

There are other ways to get people blogging too. Consider running a campaign where you ask them to write their thoughts about whatever the central topic of your book is (not about the book, but about the concept). Schedule their posts so that your readers know which site to go to, and on which day, to read the neat material that participating bloggers are creating. This is a way of sharing a target audience that grows a following for everyone participating.

If you've written a mystery novel, perhaps you ask the participating bloggers to share the best mystery novel twist they've ever read, or give them a premise and ask them to complete it.

If you've written an inspirational book, create a post on your blog asking them to share their thoughts about what your topic means in their lives, or to nominate people in their lives who they see as displaying those attributes. It's a great way to uplift others, while promoting the very concept behind your book.

I would also recommend posting a "call for reviewers" in applicable LinkedIn groups. If you don't have a LinkedIn profile, I would highly recommend creating one (as will be discussed later in this plan). Once your profile is set, you'll want to search for groups in LinkedIn that are either specific to book reviewers, book promotions, or to the industry or topic you have written about.

Who is your ideal audience? Look for those people on LinkedIn. Find the groups they participate in, and start a discussion asking for interested reviewers to contact you directly with their relevant information. (If you're mailing a copy of the book to them, you'll need their mailing address. If you can deliver it to them via an eBook format or .pdf, you'll need their e-mail address. If you can provide either one, ask them which they prefer. I have found that most reviewers prefer to get a copy in their hands as quickly as possible, and will therefore accept a digital copy. This saves you time and money in getting the book to them, so make haste and respond to their reply!)

As you spend time on different bloggers' sites, be sure to read what they're writing about and leave comments when appropriate. Whenever you comment on a blog post on someone else's website, use the available feature to leave a link to your site. This creates links that can become valuable to the visibility of your website. Make sure that you don't use the link in the comment text itself, but in the field provided. If you insert it into the comment text, your comment may be flagged as spam and never get posted. For it to be accepted, it has to either be entered into the correct field or be exceedingly relevant to the comment you're sharing.

I'll add this additional resource with a word of caution. I have not used it myself, nor have any of my clients. I came across it during a recent conversation on LinkedIn and bookmarked it because it looks incredibly useful. The problem is, I have no idea how old it is or how current it is kept. But, here it is. It's a Google doc called "Bloggers Who Interview Authors."[25] It's a running list that gives the blogger's name, a URL and what genres they deal with. There are currently 96 blogs listed at the time of this writing. Even if only half of them are still current, it's a great place to start your blogger outreach if you're willing to put a little sweat equity into the research.

A final word on the subject of finding others to do a blog review... When you ask for a review, trust your book

---

[25] alewebsocial.com/BloggersWhoInterview

to speak for itself. Asking someone else for a review is a walk of faith. You have no control over whether their review will be favorable or negative, or how much visibility that review will receive (although you should participate in promoting the review as much as you can).

Understand that a huge part of marketing your book online requires you to have faith in yourself and the words you have written. If they have merit, reviewers will see that and laud it, even if there are some negative comments thrown into their review.

Most blogging reviewers are human too, and will be respectful in the views that they post, although they'll be honest about them too. Not everyone is going to like what you've written. So, remember to take any review with a grain of salt, at the same time as looking for the nugget of truth in everything that's written about your book. That will better prepare you for your next book!

And, speaking of your next book, as you gain more of a following, you can actually create a sense of urgency and an enthusiasm to blog about your new book by limiting the number of blogging reviewers you'll accept. Michael Hyatt did this with his book *Platform: Get Noticed in a Noisy World.* [26] He announced to his mailing list that he was going to randomly choose 100 people to review his new book. He ended up with 760 volunteers, all eager to read and write about it. While you probably won't end up with hundreds of people clamoring to review your book, you never know!

Whatever you do, do not make the mistake of asking to exchange reviews with a blogger. It is highly unprofessional, and puts the other person in a bad position. If you want to offer to review someone else's book, that should be a standalone offer with no connection to whether or not they'll return the favor. The same goes for liking other authors' Facebook pages, following their social profiles, etc. It is a sure indicator of

---

[26] alewebsocial.com/Platform

an amateur when someone makes the request to exchange visibility. What if their book isn't up to your standards? What will you write in your review?

I had someone like my Facebook recently and inform me by private message that he'd done so, letting me know that he'd welcome me doing the same. Now, my latest book is an inspirational book in which I share with my readers that I hold Christian values. His book was a fictionalized story about a man's encounter with a dominatrix and his awakening awareness of sexual desires she triggers in him.

It's unlikely that our target market is the same. To like his page would simply be trying to "game the system" by increasing the number of his followers, at the same time as possibly tarnishing my brand based on what my readers expect from me.

His book is probably very well written and will appeal to certain readers. After all, he's another finalist in a book award we're competing for. So I'm not questioning the quality of his work. I'm simply pointing out that there's probably not much of an overlap in our readership, so it doesn't benefit either of us for him to like my page or me to like his. It simply confuses our readers as to what to expect from us.

So, don't pursue link or review exchanges. If you decide that you want to review a book that's been written by someone who has reviewed yours, that's fine. But don't make it contingent on them providing you with a review.

Review Sites

In addition to doing your own research to identify potential reviewers, I also recommend spending a good amount of time on review sites. These are sites that connect authors and publishers with reviewers. Depending on the site, reviews may be paid or volunteer.

The main difference is, with the paid sites, there's often some name recognition that goes along with the review, which lends authority to what's being said. But you have no control over what the review itself says, which is good; you want an honest and authentic review. When Kirkus Reviews[27] gives your book a positive review, it bears more weight than when Billy Bob Jones does. That's not to say that Billy Bob doesn't know his stuff. He may. But no one's ever heard of him before, so he has no credibility of his own to lend to the review.

Publishers Weekly[28] and its self-publishing offshoot, BookLife,[29] offer reviews, but there's no guarantee that they will review your book. If you're a self-publisher, you can submit your book for review consideration on BookLife for free. There's no guarantee that your book will be accepted, but no risk in submitting it either. So it's

---

[27] alewebsocial.com/Kirkus

[28] alewebsocial.com/PW

[29] alewebsocial.com/BookLife

worth taking the time to complete a profile and walk through the process. Books that are accepted will have their review appear in the pages of Publishers Weekly, on publishersweekly.com, and on many major bookselling sites, including Amazon, Barnes & Noble, the Apple iBookstore, and Google Play Books. BookLife reviews will also be reprinted in Publishers Weekly monthly PW Select supplement. So it can be a lot of great visibility for your book, assuming you've written a worthy read.

If you're traditionally published, have your publisher submit the title for you according to the submission guidelines. Once again, there's no guarantee that Publishers Weekly will accept your book for review, or that the review will be favorable if it is, but the distribution of the review if it is run is wide. So, it can be a great help in getting the word out about your book.

The general submission guidelines for Publishers Weekly highlight one of the reasons why your marketing plan is so important. Their first requirement is that submissions must be sent three months, preferably four, prior to the 1st day of the month of publication. Library Journal[30] has a similar requirement. If you don't plan out your marketing, you miss opportunities like this simply because you won't know early enough to account for it in your schedule.

While the review sites mentioned thus far go a long way toward getting your book in front of librarians, journalists and possibly even the media, it's also important to develop a strategy for adding reviews to the retail sites that are selling your book. I tend to focus first and foremost on Amazon, simply because that's where the majority of the online sales will most likely take place, but even then, it's important to note that a review left on Amazon.com is not displayed on your book listing on any of Amazon's international sites. So, you want to make sure that your plan accounts for adding reviews to other

---

[30] alewebsocial.com/LibraryJournal

relevant Amazon sites as well. (If you weren't aware that there are other Amazon sites, you might want to visit Amazon International[31] to learn more.)

Although I haven't tried it yet, I've heard that LibraryThing.com is another great source to find independent reviewers. It's a website that allows people to catalog their personal libraries, discover new books and connect with others who share their tastes. It also has an Early Reviewer program[32] that helps publishers distribute advance copies of books to interested readers. The publisher provides books, members sign-up to request them, and then LibraryThing matches up books with members based on the rest of their LibraryThing catalog. In the end, members get books, publishers get reviews, and LibraryThing plays matchmaker. For now, this service is completely free. So, it's well worth giving it a try and you are given a list of the e-mail addresses for

---

[31] alewebsocial.com/AMZInternational
[32] alewebsocial.com/LibraryThing

all of your reviewers so that you can keep in touch with them.

Another reviewing resource with a long-established history is the Midwest Book Review. [33] Volunteer reviewers there will review your book, CD or DVD free of charge. If you'd prefer to send an eBook, pre-publication manuscripts, galleys, uncorrected proofs, advance review copies (ARCs) and pdf files, you can pay a $50 fee to have your book reviewed in those formats. Be aware though, since books are reviewed by volunteers, there's no guarantee that a reviewer will be available to review your book even if it's passed the initial screening and been accepted for review, since only it will only be reviewed by one reviewer.

If you don't mind piecing together your reviews one site at a time, then you can also submit your book to Readers' Favorite, where a volunteer reviewer will offer

---

[33] alewebsocial.com/Midwest

your book a rating from 1 to 5-stars, and you get a nice website badge to go with it. Given the popularity of the Readers Favorite brand, a 5-star review is considered a coveted thing.

Another lesser-known place to find reviewers is BookRooster.[34] While it's not a free service (currently costs $67), BookRooster works with its list of volunteer reviewers to ensure that you get 10 honest reviews from everyday readers, not professional reviewers. This can make the look and feel of your reviews more authentic instead of scholarly.

Another popular listing site is BookBub. The site is very selective about the books it accepts, and charges a fee that's directly based on which category you want to list it for and whether you intend to offer it to BookBub subscribers for free or to charge a nominal fee for it.

---

[34] alewebsocial.com/BookRooster

Assuming your book is accepted by BookBub and that you run your campaign correctly, it can generate a great amount of exposure for you. You can learn more about the firsthand experience of British crime author Geraldine Evans on my website, where she shares the ins and outs of her BookBub experience.[35]

One of my favorite places to find new reviewers is StoryCartel.com. The focus here is more on getting people to leave honest reviews on Amazon, Goodreads and other sites, but some participants are also willing to blog about your book as well.

The way it works is, you post your book for free on Story Cartel for a limited period of time (3 weeks). Readers download your book in exchange for an honest review. To encourage readers to follow through, for every review they leave on a site you request, they receive one entry into a monthly drawing where Story Cartel gives

---

[35] alewebsocial.com/BookBub

away Kindle eReaders, Amazon and Barnes & Noble gift cards, and bestselling print books to the Story Cartel community.

To cover the cost of these prizes, each author pays $30 for every book they launch on the site. So, if you're doing one book launch, it's $30. If you have a second title or want to do a second launch period later, it's another $30. Simple! The nice thing is, it doesn't matter how old the title is. So, you can submit a book for reviews even if it's already been out for a couple of years.

As an author, you are given a list of the e-mails of everyone who downloads the book during the review period. This enables you to follow up with them, even after the download period is finished. It's a great way to connect with and grow your reading audience.

You can learn a bit more about how I ran a successful Story Cartel campaign for one of my books on my website, along with a summary of the final results of my campaign.[36]

If you're looking for reviewers that accept ARCs, consider listing your book with the Advanced Reviewers Club.[37]

There's also an unofficial Google document online called "Where Writers Win's Ultimate List of Book Review Websites."[38] I have no idea how well-maintained the document is, but it contains a list of 67 different sites where you can find reviewers. Work your way through the list and be diligent about checking into the details of each to make sure it's reputable and worthwhile. If this list isn't enough for you, you can also Google "list of book reviewers" to find additional articles and resources that will point you in the right direction.

---

[36] alewebsocial.com/SCPosts
[37] alewebsocial.com/ARC
[38] alewebsocial.com/UltimateList

You can also look for the top reviewers on Amazon, then research the genres that they review, and solicit reviews from appropriate potential reviewers. You can either start with the reviewers that are in the Amazon Hall of Fame[39] or just look at the top reviewers on Amazon. [40]

While you're at it, you may also want to see if you can request reviewers through your publisher using a website called NetGalley.com. This site has a ready membership of reviewers primed and waiting for good content to read and write about, as does Published.com. Published.com is free, so it may not grant you the same level of exposure or service. Your publisher may also have other similar sites they can recommend as well, so don't hesitate to ask them!

---

[39] alewebsocial.com/AMZHall
[40] alewebsocial.com/AMZTop

It's important to note though that when you list your title on some of these sites, you'll be charged a much larger listing fee than on Story Cartel. Currently, for NetGalley, there is a one-time fee of $399 and your title is available for up to 6 months on the site.

So look into the details carefully as you decide which sites you want to list your book with. Consider things like how many reviewers are registered with them (NetGalley has close to 200,000 registered reviewers), what promotion services they offer, are the reviews from professionals or enthusiastic readers, when do they want to see the book (pre-release, within a few months, after a year), etc. Once you've gathered all of the relevant information, then you can plan accordingly to get the most out of your efforts and budget.

Affiliates

Often, when you have a reviewer who really likes your book, they may ask if they can sell your book as an affiliate marketer. While this requires some coordination on your part, it can become a very effective means of increasing your sales.

You can even broaden your exposure to others who want to become affiliates for your book by posting your product on JVZoo,[41] ClickBank,[42] eJunkie[43] and ShareaSale,[44] and providing relevant "ad copy" or banner images for them to have on their websites. Each sale that comes from their site, results in a percentage of the sale going to them. (Personally, I like working with JVZoo the best because it handles refunds more smoothly than the other sites.)

So, affiliate networks are definitely an option to consider, if it makes sense for your genre, since the amount of work required on your part is minimal

---

[41] alewebsocial.com/JVZoo
[42] alewebsocial.com/ClickBank
[43] alewebsocial.com/Ejunkie
[44] alewebsocial.com/ShareaSale

compared to the potential exposure you'll get from the wider platform.

The one thing to keep in mind if you're going to entice affiliates to help you sell your book is that you'll want to provide them with a clean, crisp sales page. You don't want to direct affiliate links back to your website, where readers get to know more about you and your book. You want to send them to a sales page that asks questions that hook your readers, touts the benefits of your book to the prospective buyer, and offers testimonials of those who have read your book already. This is especially useful for "how to" books, but can be used for almost any kind of book.

Another means of leveraging the interest of others to sell your book is to consider offering bulk-buying discounts. Identify those companies, associations, clubs, etc. that might be interested in purchasing multiple copies of your book. This allows you to sell more copies at one time, making good use of your sales efforts. For example, if you've written a medical thriller, consider connecting with medical sales reps. They often provide clients with small gifts. Your book could be just that unusual touch that sets them apart and helps their clients remember them.

Podcasts, Live Chats, Webinars and Teleseminars

You may find that as you connect with bloggers, some may be more interested in interviewing you than in reviewing your book. Be open to any opportunity that can serve as a platform for promotion. Many bloggers who do interviews are also podcasters or regularly hold webinars and teleseminars and, depending on your personality, you may find this is an ideal forum for you.

With the advent of internet radio, Skype and Google Hangouts, it becomes easier all the time to grant interviews that reach audiences all over the world! Consider spending some time on BlogTalkRadio.com to familiarize yourself with podcasts and how they work. Then, attend a few teleseminars and webinars to see what they're like.

If you have an extensive mailing list yourself, arrange a teleseminar to talk about your book, participate as a featured guest for any book discussion groups who are reading your book, etc. You can use FreeConferenceCall.com to accommodate as many as 96 callers for up to six hours at a time, and you can record the call as well and download the recording when it's done for use on your website, etc. If you want to have both phone and computer access options for attendees, you can use InstantTeleseminar[45] instead.

Listeners enjoy the interactivity of live video chats, teleseminars, podcasts, etc. and the opportunity to offer replays and downloads enables this one-time effort to have a residual impact on the marketing of your book.

––––––––––––––––––

[45] alewebsocial.com/InstantTeleseminar

Using a Google Hangout on Air[46] to schedule an event in advance and then streaming it live to YouTube where it can be recorded and stored for long-term use can expose you to readers who have never heard of you before. These events can simultaneously be livestreamed to your Facebook page using an app called 22Social.[47] Settings in the app allow you to require attendees to like your page to see the event, thus increasing your Facebook following.

Another great feature of 22Social is that other 22Social users can clone your event, allowing them to livestream it on their page at the same time, offering you greater exposure while granting them the prestige of having you as "a guest" on their page.

When you hold a Hangout, I also recommend having the presentation played on your website. You can do this

---

[46] alewebsocial.com/Hangouts
[47] alewebsocial.com/22Social

using a plugin that was recently renamed to "RunClick," but was originally called "The Hangout Plugin" by Walt Bayliss.[48] This extends the powerful functionality of a Google Hangout by providing you with a presentation platform where people can register for your Hangout, which is integrated into your auto-responder system, capturing e-mail addresses for you and sending out reminder notices before the event and thank you notices with links to the replay afterward.

So, the way I would set things up is, use RunClick to schedule the Hangout (rather than Hangout on Air) and provide a registration platform. Once you have that all set up, use the links to that Hangout to create your presentation page on Facebook using 22Social. When you create a Register Now button on the 22Social page, link it to the RunClick presentation page.

------

[48] alewebsocial.com/RunClick

Attendees can watch it in either place, allowing you to promote it using both Facebook and your website, while growing your mailing list and Facebook following all at the same time.

Getting back to podcasts and seminars though, if you don't already have your own, find people who do, and see if you can arrange to be on their show. They are often looking for guests who will appeal to their audience, so if you position yourself as someone the audience will enjoy or benefit from hearing from, you're sure to land the show. Ultimately, this increases your exposure to the online community. It gets your name out there and enables you to share what your book is about.

I recommend subscribing to RadioGuestList.com, which sends out a regular newsletter announcing which radio shows are looking for what type of guest expert. If the whole concept of radio, internet radio and podcasting is new to you, consider ordering their MP3 series on How to Get Radio Interviews[49] for more information.

These kinds of interviews are great because people can download them to listen to them on the go and so aren't locked into being on the computer to learn more about you and your book. Recorded webinars can also be saved to YouTube and your website and linked to from your social profiles.

Additionally, people tend to find replays *long after* they were recorded. So, it leaves a nice "digital footprint" behind that will help people find you and your book for months to come, long beyond the initial launch. They can also be used as an incentive for your mailing list in the future.

When you are going to be live online, be sure to let your readers know ahead of time so that they can tune in and listen. This generates new listeners for the host show,

---

[49] alewebsocial.com/RadioGuestListAudio

which is great for them, at the same time that they are exposing you to a broader audience through their existing listeners.

After the podcast, webinar or teleseminar is over, if the show's host allows it, post a copy on your website and Facebook page so that people can come back and listen to it again at a later date or download it for their personal library.

Many podcasts are also downloadable on iTunes. So, find out whether that's the case for any shows that you are on; once again, so that you can let your readers know.

If you have rights to the material, consider having a transcription made that you can offer as a free download for people who opt-in to your mailing list. This is another way to leverage the same material and create a larger impact from this single effort. This is one of those times when you may want to consider using Speechpad.com again to outsource transcribing the audio.

Book Retail Sites

There are many sites that you can sell your book on. Of course, Amazon comes to mind, and for good reason. The site still dominates book distribution across all publishing market segments, but by a steadily decreasing margin. So, focus initially on building up your presence on Amazon, but don't neglect other sites that may form an important part of your marketing campaign, like Barnes and Noble's bn.com and ebooks.com.

Amazon

Many new authors are unaware of the fact that Amazon has a section called "Author Central" that allows you to create what's called an "author page." This is a page within Amazon that contains any information you choose to share about yourself. It links to all the books you are selling on Amazon, and appears in the Amazon search results when someone searches for your name. This can be designed as a robust landing page that you can send your readers to in order to learn more about you and what you've written.

You can include your bio, a photo, a video, and the titles you've written. Therefore, I strongly recommend that you create an author page for yourself, if you don't have one already. Be sure to include links to your website and any other social presences you may have online.

For each of your book listings, ensure that the description is complete and that the book is appropriately tagged. This enables people searching for books like yours to find yours more easily!

You can also edit the Book Extras (maintained on Shelfari) to include additional tidbits of information that are displayed in the Kindle book, like series information, character descriptions, settings and important places, memorable quotes, and more. Unfortunately, these extras are not typically available on your book's product listing page on Amazon yet. They are part of the in-book experience when a reader has already downloaded your book and started reading it.

Encourage the online community you already have (not just friends and family) to write Amazon reviews on your book page. Potential buyers will often look at the reviews to make a final buying decision. So, you want to make sure there's some good content there. Remember, "ask and you shall receive."

Once you've completed your Amazon author page, remember that there are international Amazon sites[50] as well. So go and repeat the process on whichever ones you're interested in having a presence on.

Along that same vein, Amazon has its own editorial review team as well. Submit your book to the team for consideration in the Best Books programs (Best Books of the Month and Best Books of the Year) and for possible coverage on the Amazon Books blog, Omnivoracious.com.

---

[50] alewebsocial.com/AMZInternational

When this book was first released in May 2012, the address to send your book to for consideration was:

Amazon Books Editorial Team
333 Boren Ave. N
Seattle, WA 98109

However, that information seems to have been removed from the website since then. It had previously been located in the Author, Publisher and Vendor guidelines found in Amazon's FAQ. [51] So you may need to do some research to ensure you have the most current mailing address.

There are so many things you can do where Amazon is concerned. However, once your author page and book listings are complete, I recommend saving things like participating in discussions until you've covered some of the more major tasks (like establishing your social profiles). Once you've got your online presence solidified,

---

[51] alewebsocial.com/AMZGuidelines

come spend some time on the Amazon site and learn all that it has to offer.

For example, you can start a discussion among people visiting your Amazon author page or book listing, or seek out a discussion that's already taking place in Amazon around a topic you have something to say about! (You may want to join the Meet Our Authors forum,[52] where shameless plugs for your new book are welcomed.)

Or you may want to create a Listmania list.[53] Any Amazon user can create lists of favorite books (up to 40) that will appear on your profile page and other places on the site. You could create a list of what you're reading now, of favorite classics, of books that had a profound effect on you, of "best reads of 2014..." The ideas are only limited by your imagination.

---

[52] alewebsocial.com/AMZForum
[53] alewebsocial.com/AMZListmania

Once again, it comes down the fact that new content and other forms of activity increase your visibility on the site and by association your book.

An important thing to consider if your book is available in an eBook format is whether you want to participate in the Kindle Direct Publishing[54] platform's kdpselect program. This allows you to distribute your book through the Kindle Owners' Lending Library and reach the growing number of US Amazon Prime members. Amazon gives you tools that enable you to promote your book for free. Rather than selling the eBook through this program, Amazon Prime members borrow the book and Amazon pays authors through a split of the monthly royalties it has. Per the Amazon website:

> Your share of the Kindle Owners' Lending Library Fund is calculated based on a share of the total number of qualified borrows of all participating KDP titles. For example, if the monthly fund amount is $500,000 and

---

[54] alewebsocial.com/KDP

the total qualified borrows of all participating KDP titles is 100,000 in December and if your book was borrowed 1,500 times, you will earn 1.5% (1,500/100,000 = 1.5%), or $7,500 in December.

While the numbers they show in the example sound exciting, you have to keep in mind that you could just as easily only have 15 borrows, and earn $75 for the month. And the reader can't simply just borrow it, they have to get at least 10% of the way through the book for it to be a qualified "borrow."

In exchange for participating in this program for 90 days, you cannot distribute your book digitally anywhere else, including on your website. However, you can continue to distribute your book in physical format wherever you'd like. So, there's a trade-off there.

You're given the tools you need to promote it. You can still sell the Kindle version (and your print version) on Amazon during the period of exclusivity. It's just that all eBook sales must be done on the Amazon platform. Only you can decide whether it's worth it to you or not.

Barnes and Noble

The same comments about book listings on Amazon apply to book listings on the Barnes and Noble website. Be sure that your listing is complete and accurate.

Ask readers to post reviews. Never under-estimate the influence ratings have on your book sales. The better the ratings, the more sales you'll see. And the more reviews you have, the more objective the ratings are. So, start collecting those as soon as you can.

The Barnes and Noble website does not have the same "underground" culture that Amazon has. There are no discussion groups, Listmania lists, or other features that encourage engagement on the site, which is disappointing. But you do have the option of requesting that they create a Meet the Writers[55] page for you. Unfortunately, much of the control of that page is

---

[55] alewebsocial.com/B&NPage

retained by Barnes and Noble, so you can't simply go in and update it whenever you want like on Amazon.

What Barnes and Noble *does* offer that Amazon can't, is the opportunity to request being considered for an author event.[56] Each year, they host more than 28,000 author events across the U.S. These appearances are great ways for authors to gain exposure and build their profiles in local communities, while allowing readers to meet and speak with their favorite authors.

eBook Distribution

As stated earlier in this book, 85% of eBooks produced are created *in addition* to printed books. But where do you market them? Typically, they are offered right alongside their printed counterparts. But what if the only format you're offering your book in is an eBook format?

There are a few different options there. Obviously, you can still publish the book to Amazon. However, if you

---

[56] alewebsocial.com/B&NEvent

enroll in the kdpselect program, you have to wait 90 days to market your eBook elsewhere. Once the period of exclusivity is over though, you're welcome to sell and distribute your eBook anywhere you'd like.

Alternatively, you can skip participating in the Lending Library program and publish your eBook to Amazon still. No exclusivity is needed there.

Amazon actually makes it very easy for you to create a Kindle-ready book. The simplest way that I found was to take an existing manuscript (in Word or .pdf form) and send it to my own Kindle using the Send to Kindle[57] program. Once I synced my Kindle and downloaded the newly formatted book, I connected the Kindle to my computer using the USB cord that came with it, and copied the book from the Kindle to my computer. While there seem to be many other methods for creating a Kindle-ready book, this was the easiest one to do.

---

[57] alewebsocial.com/SendtoKindle

If you are offering your book for sale on Amazon and you make a Kindle version available, I strongly recommend that you register your book on the Authorgraph.com site as well. This affords purchasers of your eBook the opportunity to ask you to autograph their copy. To learn more about how to offer Authorgraphs, refer to "Personalizing the eBook Experience." [58] (NOTE: When Authorgraph was first released, it was called "Kindlegraph" instead, which is how this article refers to it.)

Additionally, if you're a self-published author, you can join Amazon's Publisher Participation program, and set up your book so that it can be "searched inside." This allows readers to look at selected pages of your book based on keywords they enter without having to purchase it first.

---

[58] alewebsocial.com/Authorgraph

For any other eBook format (for a Nook, iPad, etc.), you want to create an ePub file. I use a free piece of software called Calibre[59] to make ePub copies of my manuscript. While it allows you to create both ePub, Kindle and other digital formats of your book, I have found that the SendToKindle process works best for creating the Kindle versions, and only use Calibre to create the ePub versions and check the results.

So, in addition to offering your eBook on your own website, as well as on Kindle, Nook and iPad, other sites allow you to post your eBook too. Currently, ebooks.com is a very popular site. It bills itself as "the world's leading source of eBooks." This is a good site to go to in order to further promote non-Kindle formatted eBooks. However, they do not work directly with authors and require a publisher to contact them on your behalf. Their explanation is that they focus on a selection of high

---

[59] alewebsocial.com/Calibre

volume popular and academic publishers to work with. Their recommendation if you want your eBook posted on their site is to work with an aggregator instead in the hopes that they may be able to get your book listed there. You can read a review of some current aggregators in "12 Sites for eBook Publishing" [60] to see if there's one that's right for you.

Repurpose Your Content

There are many ways to repurpose content. Typically you hear this term in relation to content on your website. (Make a video. Strip the audio out for a podcast. Transcribe it for a blog post. Gather multiple blog posts together as a summary post or free eBook that you offer in exchange for building your mailing list, also referred to as a "loss leader" in the sales industry.)

---

[60] alewebsocial.com/12Sites

However, with publishing, repurposing your content means finding other ways to distribute it. The top 3 that come to mind are whether you offer your book as a hardcover, paperback or eBook. But you can also take that same content, have it recorded (or record it yourself) and distributed as an audiobook. Or you can have your talk that's related to the book videotaped and packaged as a DVD. Both audiobooks and DVDs can be offered as physical products or as digital downloads.

You may also consider creating a workbook or small group study guide from the material to encourage people to dig deeper into the content you've created and spend more time with it.

Many authors are now having their own mobile app developed to enable people to interact directly with them and their content easily from a mobile device. Remember the trend we spoke about earlier? Most internet access will be from mobile devices in the future, which opens up a whole new search engine to us. Instead of just focusing on getting found on Google and on social networks, you also need to consider how you're going to position yourself to be found for what you write about and do in mobile app directories.

Think about the days of the Westward Expansion. Those individuals who got there first got to stake out the largest claims to territory. It's the same when an entirely new search engine appears. Those who can claim the best keywords and hold them securely will get the lion's share of the exposure.

There are all sorts of ways to offer up your content to potential readers that meet their specific learning styles and needs. And each becomes another revenue-generating stream for you. But it's not just going to happen. You have to plan for it and do the necessary research to make your mark.

Audiobooks

If you're interested in having your book made into an audiobook, you need to decide whether you're going to narrate it yourself or hire a voice-over artist to do it for you. While it's easy to think you can do a good job of it yourself, there is a knack to doing voice-over work, not to mention having the right equipment to create a quality recording.

I recommend that you work with a professional to create your audiobook, unless you are trained in voice-over techniques and have the proper equipment or studio space you can rent.

Many authors are familiar with Amazon's CreateSpace platform that enables them to become their own self-publishers. But not as many are familiar with Amazon's ACX platform,[61] which allows authors to partner with voice-over artists and producers to create audio recordings. This can even be done with no initial budget by offering a royalty split to your voice-over artist and producer. Just be certain to look through the legal

---

[61] alewebsocial.com/ACX

documents associated with the project to be clear about how everything will work moving forward. (That should always be the case whenever you're doing any kind of publishing. Be clear about what rights you are granting the publisher and which you're retaining for yourself. You don't want to find your distribution options limited by selecting a publishing option that doesn't meet your needs.)

Once your audiobook is completed, ACX makes it available for sale at Audible, on Amazon and on iTunes.

If you choose to record your own audiobook or produce it without using ACX, there are still ways to get the completed product on Amazon and iTunes so that you're using them for distribution. But you will be responsible for all of the other aspects of the production yourself. While it can be a big project to do, once you've worked your way through the process a time or two, it becomes much easier to manage.

At Aleweb Social Marketing, we have frequently taken prepared recordings and videos, edited and remixed them, added intros and outros, and then published them using a service like Kunaki[62] to create CDs and DVDs that can be added to an eCommerce site along with their digital download versions.

It's not hard to do once you figure it all out. The question is, is it the best use of your time to do it yourself? Sometimes, the answer is "yes," and sometimes it's "no." You'll need to decide that for yourself.

Social Media

Social media allows us to catch up with friends we haven't seen in years, and it also provides us with a way to gain new contacts with and through like-minded

---

[62] alewebsocial.com/Kunaki

people. But it's the way we get our information that makes social media so special.

Unlike traditional forms of media, you are able to interact with the information you're given. You can make comments on a news story to let your voice be heard, you can share that news story with others, and you can even create your own content that can be shared in the same way.

That's the power of social media, and that's why it's so very important to establish a presence for you and your book on social networks.

When you do, make sure that the branding of your social profiles carries over or ties in to your website. A visitor should be able to go from your website to Facebook to Pinterest to Twitter to YouTube and Google+ and still tell that it's all related to the same thing. This means ensuring that the colors, images, and "feel" of each are consistent. If you're uncertain how to do this yourself, it's worthwhile to work with a graphic artist to develop the background and images that make for a seamless platform for your book.

Here in *The Plan*, I'm just going to cover a few of the more commonly used social networks, but do your research. Know the target demographic you're trying to reach and what their social media habits are. For example, if you're looking to connect with a younger audience, you may need to consider using Instagram rather than Facebook and SnapChat and Vine instead of YouTube. So, do your due diligence before getting started. Don't waste your time building an outpost on a social platform your readers don't visit.

If you need additional help in getting started, take a look at The Bite-Sized Marketer.[63] This subscription service teaches you how to market yourself online one bite at a time using short weekly video tutorials that you can implement in an hour or less of your time each week.

---

[63] alewebsocial.com/BSM

Facebook

Did you know that there are over 152 million daily active Facebook users in the U.S. and Canada alone, and that the average user spends 18 minutes on Facebook each time they visit? Facebook also ranks second only to Google in terms of its web traffic. Knowing that, you'd think it's a clear decision to build a Facebook community, which requires building a page. However, Facebook is making it increasingly more difficult to get the content from your page in front of people without paying for advertising or to boost your posts. So don't put all your eggs in the Facebook basket!

That's not to say "Ignore Facebook." People will search for and find you on Facebook and it's good to have a presence there. Just don't expect it to be the only place they can find you or you'll be limiting your visibility severely.

For your page, you'll want to start first by creating visually stimulating graphics, photos and potentially some video. It's worth hiring a graphic artist to make sure what you end up with is high-quality and professional-looking.

After you create your page in Facebook and fill in all the relevant details about yourself and your book, you may want to create a separate landing page.

Prior to Facebook implementing the Timeline format for pages, it was possible to send non-fans to a different part of your page than people who were already fans. Fans were sent to the wall, while non-fans could be sent to a specially designed "landing page" that often looked more like a website than a Facebook page.

After the Timeline format was implemented, you couldn't automatically differentiate between fans and non-fans anymore. Everyone goes to the wall now. But you *can* still creating landing pages and send people directly to this part of your page using e-mail and social media links, or even links on your own wall. Each landing page has its own URL (separate from your page's wall), and when you invite people to follow you on Facebook, you can use this URL instead of the page's.

When you create a landing page, you want it to be engaging and to include an e-mail sign-up or offer a free download. (This is an ideal way to build your mailing list.) And you want a clear call to action to "like" your page.

Or you may decide to use a recording from an earlier Google Hangout as an enticement to follow you. You can do that using the 22Social app I mentioned earlier.

In developing a landing page, you may decide that you want a professional developer to help you. However, there are many apps out there that consist of a template you can select and set up yourself. If you use a free app, you are often limited to only one custom page, but you may find that's all you need to get started.

Be sure to set your "vanity URL" for the page. This replaces the Facebook-generated URL, which consists of a bunch random numbers and letters, with an easy-to-communicate and remember URL that contributes to your visibility to the search engines as well! For example, my professional page is facebook.com/tara.r.alemany, which can also be shortened to fb.com/tara.r.alemany. Nice and easy to remember!

You'll also want to set up a feed from your blog so that each time you post on your blog, it's "fed" directly to your Facebook wall. This way, your Facebook community will always know when there's a new reason to return to your website. NetworkedBlogs[64] and Social RSS[65] are commonly used apps for this purpose.

Facebook also provides various social plugins to integrate your website and its network together. Be sure to look through them, decide which ones you like best, and then make them part of your website. If you used the Ecwid plugin on your website or set up a MailChimp opt-in, you can integrate those things into your Facebook

---

[64] alewebsocial.com/NetworkedBlogs
[65] alewebsocial.com/SocialRSS

page as well, enabling followers to learn about your books, buy your products and join your mailing list without ever leaving Facebook.

For an up-to-date list of the currently available social plugins, visit Facebook's Developers site[66].

Some people choose to add something like the Facebook Comments app[67] to their website, where appropriate. It enables people to engage with your website content, while sharing that information on their own Facebook profile. This will generate more visibility for your site since the comments they share aren't limited just to your website visitors. When you are replying to comments using this app, you can reply either as yourself (your profile) or as your brand (your page). I recommend replying as your page, as this will bring more traffic to your Facebook page as well. (Otherwise, you

---

[66] alewebsocial.com/FacebookDevelopers
[67] alewebsocial.com/FacebookComments

may find yourself getting friend requests from people you'd much rather have following your page.)

In addition to making announcements online that you can now be found on Facebook, you should also create a small poster that can be used at your author events, speaking engagements, and book signings. It should include the "call to action" to "Follow Us on Facebook" and be prominently displayed on your product table. These are very effective means of building a following right then and there.

When you design the poster, be sure to include the URL of your page for mobile users, a QR code that automatically lets them join your page for smartphone users, and instructions on where to send a text message to follow your page for cell phone users. Make it a visually engaging poster branded specifically for you and your book.

To create your own QR codes for your poster or any other promotional materials you may create, I recommend using QR Stuff.[68] This site allows you to define QR codes with the functionality that you want (including automatically liking your Facebook page), and then to download your code for future use.

To get people to follow your page using a text message, instruct them to "text 'like <*yourpagename*>' to 32665 from any mobile phone." In <yourpagename>, substitute the vanity part of your Facebook URL. For example, in http://www.Facebook.com/AlewebSocial, the vanity portion of the URL is "AlewebSocial." So, I would instruct people to text "like AlewebSocial" to Facebook's mobile number, 32665 (or FBOOK).

When considering what content to share on Facebook, remember that Facebook users move fast. To grab their attention, you have to respect their behavior. Think about their responses before you pose a question. Make it simple and easy for them to answer. "What's one word

---

[68] alewebsocial.com/QRStuff

that best describes x...?" Each question should be short, easy and entertaining as often as possible. This creates more engagement.

Consider: "What was the last book you read? Would you recommend it?" "I'm working on X today. What do you think about...?" "What's your best tip for _____ (related to your niche)." "Do you have a FB page? Post your link to share with the group!"

And switch up the type of content. Share links. Post pictures. Upload video. Provide short excerpts of your book. Create some of the content yourself, and share things of interest to your readers from other sources the rest of the time. A fun way to get people talking about your book is to take a screen shot of something exciting (like your stellar rise up through the Amazon rankings) and share it on Facebook.

You may also want to consider running a Facebook photo contest prior to the launch. It could be as simple as asking people to submit a photo of themselves with a sign stating "Help Me Launch" or with a copy of the book, or with some other message that's relevant to your book. The prize can be something as simple as an autographed copy of your book for them and a friend. Yet, as they participate in the contest, their friends learn about you and visibility for your new book increases. Please note though that Facebook has very strict policies regarding the running of contests. So be sure to read through them[69] carefully and consider using a tool like Rafflecopter[70] to manage the contest according to the rules.

Additionally, as you set up book-related events, you can create an event and invite your friends and followers. This enables people to see and share what you're doing, as well as providing broader visibility to the Facebook search engine for your activity.

---

[69] alewebsocial.com/FacebookGuidelines
[70] alewebsocial.com/Rafflecopter

You can even look for other pages on Facebook who have a similar target audience and start getting engaged with the community there. I'm not advocating stealing someone else's audience. But if you have a shared interest, getting to know an established audience in another venue is not a crime. You can even make it worthwhile to the page admin by offering a special deal for their audience alone.

Unfortunately, Facebook's search functionality isn't useful enough to identify the best pages to work with. (Which ones have the largest and most active following?) So, I use a special tool called "FB Lead Finder"[71] to research pages related to the topics I'm interested in. Then I begin participating on them or reach out to the admin if I want to make a special arrangement with them.

Keep in mind, if I post on another page's wall, the information ends up in a small little sidebar area called

---

[71] alewebsocial.com/FBLeadFinder

"posts by others." If the page admin posts it, it goes into the newsfeed of its followers. So, for an announcement like an event that might be of interest to the page's following, it's better to have the admin voluntarily share it than for me to post it there myself. Plus, I think it's more respectful...

Once your page is ready and you've got some content posted and conversation flowing, you may want to consider targeted Facebook advertising that increases the visibility of your page quickly. You can select a highly targeted audience (those who would be most likely to be interested in your book) and invite them to "like" your page. But always make it clear as to "what's in it for them." Don't expect them to share their precious contact details without giving them something worthwhile in exchange.

Pinterest

Pinterest is a social bookmarking site that allows people to bookmark articles, websites, videos and other online content that interests them. But instead of the bookmark being text-based as it is on Reddit, Digg, StumbleUpon and other social bookmarking sites, it's image-based.

Pinterest users create a "board" and "pin" pictures to it. Friends and followers will see the new pin and either "like," comment or "repin" it to their own boards. It's amazing how quickly information spreads on Pinterest if the images used are attention-getting enough.

While it's a newer site than Facebook, Twitter, LinkedIn or the others, its adoption rate has been faster than any social network that came before, and 85% of the content on it is repinned content (meaning someone liked what they saw there and chose to pin it to one of their own boards). So, Pinterest is not a place to be ignored.

This means that as you find images for your blog posts, you'll want to make them engaging. And as you encourage people to share pictures of themselves for the launch (with a sign, book or whatever other idea you come up with), you'll want to coordinate where those images are loaded. You can share things from Pinterest to Facebook and Twitter, but Facebook has never played nicely with its competition. So, you can't pin things from Facebook to Pinterest.

To learn a bit more about Pinterest, read "Why Pinterest Should Interest You."[72]

Remember too that Pinterest is not limited to sharing images. You can share video content as well. So make sure your book trailer is added to a board in addition to other content of interest to your readers.

Twitter

Twitter is one of my favorite social networks to find new people to engage with. Whether you want to use it to connect with other people in the literary world or interact with your readers, develop a strong brand with your Twitter account.

---

[72] alewebsocial.com/WhyPinterest

Decide early on whether the book will have its own Twitter account or if you share one with it. For a book that promotes self-improvement or societal change or engagement, having its own Twitter account can be a good thing.

However, the drawback is that your second book, should there be one, will be in direct competition with the first one for an audience later on.

Consolidating all of your books into your personal brand and differentiating between them with unique hashtags may be more beneficial in the long run. (If you're unfamiliar with hashtags, read "Hashtags Demystified..."[73])

At times though, you may determine that the community and following that's going to be built up around your book will be long-lasting and really needs to stand apart from you. This is particularly useful if there

---

[73] alewebsocial.com/Hashtags

are workshops, speaking engagements, videos and other book-related material that require a place for people engaged in the topic to communicate with one another and with you. Then, and only then, should you create a separate Twitter account for the book. (For example, The Noticer Project is based on Andy Andrews' book, *The Noticer*,[74] and calls for people to notice the five most influential people in your life now rather than waiting until a wedding, graduation or even a funeral to take notice of the special, influential people in our lives. Unfortunately, the site and social profiles have been abandoned since Dec 2012 and are now riddled with spam, but the concept was wonderful!)

When you choose your Twitter ID, you ideally want something relevant and short since it counts towards the allotted 140 characters in a retweet. A rule of thumb is, you want to keep your tweet content short enough for

---

[74] alewebsocial.com/TheNoticer

people to share. That means, you have to write less than *[140 characters - your username - 3]* ("RT" followed by a space). This enables people to share your content with their followers without having to modify what you've written. Typically, I tell my clients to aim for 120 characters or less in their tweets.

If you're having a hard time picking a Twitter ID, consider letting your readers help in the decision-making. Post a question on Facebook asking for suggestions or mail the same question out to your mailing list. If you have a couple of ideas, find out which they prefer or if they have other suggestions!

Pay attention to those on Twitter who are using the phrases related to your topic in their tweets. Those are the people you should especially try to engage with because it's what they're thinking about already. It may please and surprise them to know that there's a book out there relevant to their interest.

You could even organize a TweetChat around the hashtag you create for your book. It's a great way to gain followers as well as visibility.

You'll also want to use Twitterfeed[75] to add a blog feed to your Twitter ID. That way every time you post something new on your blog, it's automatically tweeted to your followers.

I often have my clients register their Twitter ID on multiple Twitter registration sites, as well as create a paper.li[76] daily newspaper relevant to their specific topic. Paper.li does a lot towards increasing the visibility of your profile because it automatically creates a daily newspaper published under your name and identifies the top contributors each day. Those contributors often will write to thank you for featuring them in your newspaper, which gives you visibility to their followers as well.

---

[75] alewebsocial.com/Twitterfeed
[76] alewebsocial.com/PaperLI

At the same time, I have them create a custom, branded Twitter page on Twylah.[77] While paper.li aggregates content from sources other than yourself, Twylah aggregates content that *you* have shared. It can become a very effective place for people to get a quick overview of who you are and what you're doing.

Twylah also helps you focus on using your Twitter profile as an extension of your brand by conducting a regular brand assessment. You identify the topic areas that are relevant for your brand and Twylah monitors how well you're covering those areas while making suggestions on how you can improve your Twitter usage along the way. It's a great resource for someone who's just getting started.

YouTube

Establishing a YouTube channel that includes excerpts from your book as well as your talks (if you're a

_____

[77] alewebsocial.com/Twylah

speaker) can be extremely powerful. There's a whole generation out there that loves visual content and it's great material for your website and other social channels as well.

To produce videos well will take some time and a little bit of money, but can go a long way to increasing your visibility because search engines pick up video content long before they notice text updates. There are several great apps that allow you to record, edit and produce videos right from your mobile phone that can be published directly to YouTube. Gone are the days of needing a film crew, studio and green screen, even if they do look nice.

For an example of a writer and speaker who leverages his YouTube channel well, take a look at Andy Andrews.[78] He creates "trailers" for each of his books that are engaging and really draw the viewer in, making them

---

[78] alewebsocial.com/AndyAndrews

want to get a copy of the book themselves. At the same time, he has a Questions & Answers series that allows readers to learn more about him and the topics he covers. Since he's a consummate storyteller, his channel provides his fans with stories to keep them engaged while they wait for his next book to come out.

This is a step that many authors are missing, because they tend to think of their print media as only being promotable through print methods. However, done well, promoting your book and related materials through YouTube can be a very powerful marketing vehicle.

Keep in mind that any video you create can also be transcribed. The text can be used on your website or blog, and snippets can be used on your social profiles. Additionally, when you transcribe a video, that text should be uploaded to YouTube with the video. It's great metadata to increase the visibility of your video within the YouTube search engine and, since YouTube is owned by Google, within Google as well.

Another method of creating metadata for the video is to add closed captioning to it. I recommend that my clients use a program called "MovieCaptioner" to do this. It is available for Windows[79] or Mac.[80] When you load your video into the program, it plays the video 4 seconds at a time, allowing you the opportunity to type the text that's just been read and set the positioning of when and where the text appears in the video. When it is uploaded to YouTube, it creates additional data for YouTube to process, making it easier to know which search results your particular video should be shown in, at the same time as making your video content more readily accessible to those with auditory impairments.

Each video you create can then also be uploaded to other video-hosting sites as well, simply to amplify their

---

[79] alewebsocial.com/MovieCaptionerWin
[80] alewebsocial.com/MovieCaptionerMac

reach. A great tool for that is TubeMogul's OneLoad[81] video distribution service.

If you don't have any video yet, you can start with some simple videos just to have some content. Consider creating something using Animoto[82] or finding a video animator or creator on Fiverr.[83] Let your creative juices flow and inspire your readers to want more!

As you add more videos to your YouTube channel, you can string them together in related playlists and embed them on your website. That way, instead of having a single video play on a page of your website, you can use the playlist instead. This is great for testimonials, reader comments, speaking clips, etc.

---

[81] alewebsocial.com/OneLoad
[82] alewebsocial.com/Animoto
[83] alewebsocial.com/Fiverr

LinkedIn

Many writers do not think of business networking as something that's really relevant to them, and LinkedIn is definitely geared towards business networking. But what many people do not realize is, there's a whole lot more to LinkedIn than networking!

This is a place where business professionals in all lines of work congregate to discuss shared interests, answer questions, and generally look for interesting information to read and share.

Additionally, your profile gives you the opportunity, yet again, to write information about yourself and your book that is visible to the search engines as well as to individuals.

No matter what other line of work you are in, make sure you add "Author" and the name of your book to your work experience. In your summary, include a brief description of the book and a link to further information along with whatever else you write about yourself there.

You also want to identify yourself as an author in the "headline" of your profile.

LinkedIn allows you to connect up to three websites to your profile, in addition to connecting to your Twitter profile. For instance, you could point one to your website, another to your Amazon listing and the third to a particularly glowing review or your Facebook page.

You should also update your profile URL to have a vanity URL, just as you did with Facebook. Instead of using the randomly-generated, hard-to-remember URL, changes yours to include your name. Mine is http://www.linkedin.com/in/taraalemany.

When you write your summary, write it in a conversational style. Be relaxed, but professional. I always recommend writing in the first-person (using "I"), but keep the message of the summary focused on things of value to your target audience. Let them know what it is that you have to share that's relevant or of value to them.

With over a million groups available on LinkedIn, find those relevant to your topic, join them, and start engaging in the conversations that are taking place. This becomes a fantastic resource for new connections and potential readers. You can even share information in the groups periodically about your book and your latest activities. Just make sure that you balance that with establishing real connections with individuals within the groups. Remember to be social. No bullhorns allowed!

Use Wordpress' Publicize settings to connect your blog to LinkedIn, so that new posts are shared in your LinkedIn status updates. That way, your connections can find your latest blog posts with a link back to your website. (The Publicize settings also allow you to post directly to Facebook, Twitter, Tumblr, Path and Google+.)

LinkedIn also allows you to maintain a LinkedIn blog now that is visible to your entire network and beyond, and that your connections are reminded of in the LinkedIn Pulse newsletter that they regularly receive.

Make sure that you keep your profile fresh with updated content all the time. As you make changes to it, LinkedIn sends out a weekly e-mail that enables your connections to see what it is that's new with you. Staying in front of them on a regular, non-invasive way ensures that they remember you later.

Consider adding links to book trailers, sample chapters and free downloads, as well as interviews, reviews, etc. to your profile. Make it as interesting and visual as possible.

You can use that same status update e-mail to remind you to stay connected with your network. Take a few moments each week to wish people a happy birthday, congratulate them on a work anniversary, and comment on their latest blog posts.

Also, each section of your profile is moveable. So, be certain that you're displaying the most relevant information first. At any given time, that can change. Your background (work history and education) may be particularly important one week, while your recommendations and skills may be more important the next. These are drag-and-drop modules within your profile, so feel free to move them around as you see fit.

Google+

Google+ is very similar to Facebook in many ways. While the terminology may be different, the overall functionality available is the same. As a result, people are still trying to figure out how to incorporate it into their overall online presence.

The most powerful feature of Google+ (or "G+" as some people refer to it) is its "hangouts." These are group video chat rooms that enable up to 10 people to hang out together. As I mentioned earlier, these group video conferences can be recorded to YouTube and stored there, and simulcast to Facebook using the 22Social app.

One musician, Daria Musk,[84] leveraged G+'s hangouts to have her first "world tour" all in the space of a single night. She has introduced her music to more people than she ever could have on a live concert stage, and developed a devoted following on G+, with over 3,469,000 people following her there as of the time of this writing. (Two years ago, when the first edition of this book came out, she had 297,000 people following her on G+. That's a lot of growth in 2 years!)

Daria's fans have become her ardent supporters and advisors, helping her to select the single for her next album, among other business decisions.

All of this visibility and her massive popularity led to a concert in Boston in August 2014 featuring Daria that was sponsored by AOL, Chevrolet and OnStar and was powered by the new built-in vehicle wifi in her Chevy Silverado. How cool is that?!

---

[84] alewebsocial.com/DariaMusk

As a writer, you could use hangouts to have a shared book reading, a Meet the Author session, or a number of other possibilities. You're only limited by your imagination. If you've been to a recent conference where you've met some other great authors, consider holding a Hangout together so that you can talk about what you learned at the conference, etc. while allowing your combined audiences get to know other writers. If you know the writers ahead of time, you can always do the Hangout before the conference to generate some support and visibility for what's yet to come.

So far as the other features of G+ go, they're fairly similar to Facebook, but a little cleaner. There's no advertising on it yet, although that will most likely come with time.

One of the advantages that G+ has though over Facebook is that the Google search engine indexes the posts in G+. That means that content shared in G+ can be found in Google's search results. Since Google doesn't index Facebook content, you'll never see content from Facebook appearing in search results on Google. You'll only see that a page exists, but not what's posted on it. For that reason, G+ cannot be ignored.

So go ahead and create your G+ profile and page, making sure that you use consistent branding with your other social networks and website. (Like Facebook, personal presences on the network are "profiles," and anything business-related is a "page.") Once they're created, be sure to add a +1 button[85] and badge[86] to your website, and create vanity URLs for both your profile and page using gplus.to.[87]

---

[85] alewebsocial.com/+1Button
[86] alewebsocial.com/+1Badge
[87] alewebsocial.com/GplusTo

Mobilizing Your Network

Once your social profiles are ready, you can ask your most influential friends and followers to help you promote the book and your profiles.

To do this, set up a page first on your website that's "hidden" (a page that can only be accessed if you give someone a specific link to go to; it is not part of the menu structure of the website, nor is it on the site map).

Create pre-crafted tweets, e-mail messages, Facebook posts, etc. that people can simply click or copy and paste in order to share the information with their communities. The easier you make it for them to support you, the more likely they are to do just that!

You'll also want to ensure that those tweets contain relevant hashtags that will help people who aren't even looking for you, find you.

Then send a private message to your friends and followers requesting their help promoting your book. Let them know that you've created some standardized posts

125

they can share, or they are welcome to create their own, and provide them with a link to the "hidden" page.

Always make sure that this interaction is private, and preferably made using their preferred communication platform (whether that's e-mail, phone, social network or what-have-you). But invite them to help spread the word in any way they are comfortable with.

You can also add yourself to a Triberr group of mutually supportive bloggers, and then blog about your launch efforts or book topic. To be fair though, the folks that help spread the word about your blog post need you to do the same for their posts. So, be certain that you add yourself to a tribe (or start one of your own) that you're comfortable mutually promoting!

Free eBooks

A Kindle version of a book on Amazon enables users to download the first chapter to read before they make a decision to buy. You can use this same concept to offer a free eBook sample (regardless of the format you use) to your online community. Let the book grab their attention, and they'll go looking for more. That often works well for fiction books. Alternatively, you could offer a free discussion guide to encourage and support book clubs to feature your book. (Remember? Anytime that one sale contains multiple copies of your book, you're leveraging group buying! And that's a good thing.)

For non-fiction, you may want to create a "short report," that covers the highlights of the book you want to sell, but glosses over the details. This too becomes a teaser intended to elicit a certain reaction from your reader.

This free eBook can be the "bait" that entices them to join your mailing list or to "like" your Facebook page. It can also be a give-away at events you go to, a bonus given with other purchases, a gift given to select "winners" during webinars or teleseminars, etc.

Always make sure that the eBook you give for free contains information at the end of it as to how they can purchase the rest of the book! Without a specific "call to action," don't be surprised if you get no results! Always be clear about what you want the reader to do next!

In addition, make it easy for pleased readers to share. Consider embedding a Retweet button (like the one below) at least once within your eBook.

This particular button is one used with permission from Michael Stelzner[88] of Social Media Examiner, and you can download a copy of it on the Resources page at alewebsocial.com/ThePlanResources.

Don't just limit your give-away to your own mailing list and website visitors though. Offer it as a giveaway to

---

[88] alewebsocial.com/MikeStelzner

others who have mailing lists that reach your target audience. Suggest that they send it out as a free offer in their next newsletter. It builds good will between them and their regular audience (we all like gifts!) and gets your work in front of people who may have never seen it before.

Get Listed

There are numerous websites out there that allow authors to list their books and website information in an easily searched format. Consider creating a listing on sites like Authors Den,[89] Shelfari,[90] NetGalley,[91] Goodreads[92] and Published.[93]

---

[89] alewebsocial.com/AuthorsDen
[90] alewebsocial.com/Shelfari
[91] alewebsocial.com/NetGalley
[92] alewebsocial.com/Goodreads
[93] alewebsocial.com/Published

In addition, add your title to Bowker's *Books in Print*[94] database if your publisher has not already done this for you. This database is used by retailers, libraries and schools to identify new titles that they may want to carry. This increases the awareness of your title to potential readers all over the world. Both print and digital titles qualify for this program, and the service is available to self-published and traditionally published authors alike.

Book Awards

As authors, there are two great feathers we often seek to add to our caps. The title of "bestselling author" and that of "award-winning author."

Bestselling is all about the sales numbers. What you're doing in reading this book and defining and

---

[94] alewebsocial.com/Bowkers

implementing your marketing plan is working toward creating a bestselling book.

However, the award-winning part of it requires you to submit your work to award contests.

Every contest has its own set of rules regarding its focus, criteria and fee structure. So, you'll have to search for the contests that are right for your book. But I have submitted works to both the Writer's Digest Self-Published book award[95] contest before, as well as the Readers' Favorite annual contest.[96] As a matter of fact, my book *The Best is Yet to Come*[97] received both a 5-star rating, was a finalist in multiple categories, and won an Honorable Mention in the Readers' Favorite contest, allowing me to make the claim of being an award-winning author for the first time.

---

[95] alewebsocial.com/WritersDigest
[96] alewebsocial.com/ReadersFavorite
[97] alewebsocial.com/BIYTC

And if you happen to win a book award, you might want to read "Congratulations, You Won a Book Award! Now What?"[98] to learn how get the most mileage out of it. It's a guest post on my website from the president of Readers' Favorite, James Ventrillo.

Events

When you're speaking, attending a Meet the Author session, holding a book signing, or have other public events to promote, keep a list of websites you regularly want to update. This is more than simply writing a press release. It's disseminating the information throughout your online community; posting the event on your Facebook page, announcing it in Twitter, sharing it on LinkedIn, finding online calendars for local events (Patch.com is always a great resource for that), and so on.

---

[98] alewebsocial.com/Congratulations

You can also make a listing on Eventbrite,[99] which gets your event into their directory and creates visibility in front of potential readers who might never have found you otherwise. The Eventbrite listing can then be embedded on your website to handle registrations and ticket sales.

Once you get your event information set up, ask your community to help promote it! This is where you could use another "hidden" page on your website to share pre-crafted tweets, posts and e-mail messages for people to share with their communities.

If you have developed a talk or workshop around your book, can any piece of it be done as a webinar or teleseminar? This helps to draw additional attention to the book, while building a larger community for you.

---

[99] alewebsocial.com/Eventbrite

Bestseller Campaign

Of course, the biggest event that you'll want to focus on is your bestseller campaign. You can use many of the elements laid out in this eBook to contribute to that effort.

To begin with, set a sale date for your campaign that is several weeks (maybe even a month or two) into the future. This will give you the time necessary to "rally the troops."

Depending on which bestseller list you're trying to get on, you may want to direct all sales efforts at one sales site so that your results are concentrated rather than dispersed across multiple sites (as when you're targeting an Amazon bestseller status) or spread them out across multiple sites (as when you're targeting a NYT bestseller status).

If you're focusing your attention on Amazon, direct all sales there. During the course of the sale day, you'll be able to easily track your efforts through the site. In addition, other bestseller lists pay attention to bestsellers on Amazon as potentially interesting to their readers as well.

However, if you're focusing your attention on something like the NYT bestseller list, you need to keep up a concerted effort and make a large number of sales at a variety of retailers over the course of a week. (Amazon tracks its bestsellers by the hour.)

Next, create a marketing plan that lays out all of the tactics from this book that you plan to implement. Determine what you can do yourself and what you'll need additional resources for, then secure those additional resources.

Planning and coordination is crucial to make your bestseller campaign a success. So, don't neglect this aspect of it. Consider having all of your blogging reviewers post their reviews in the week leading up to the sale, especially if you're taking pre-sale orders. (Pre-sales count toward the sales figures on the launch day, but are often only available to books being traditionally published. Currently, Amazon does not allow self-publishers to take pre-sales.)

Be clear about your financial goals for the book and the budget (both financial and temporal) you have to work with so that you can identify the best marketing tactics for you. Then, like Jack Canfield recommended, do 5 things to promote your book every day. It doesn't matter how big or small they are. Take action. Keep moving. Do it again.

As the marketing plan takes shape, I like to use a project-management tool like Trello[100] to keep track of what needs to be done, what's currently being done and what's already done. This information can be shared with multiple people, giving you a clear view on what everyone is doing. Due dates and reminders help you to keep on top of the most important things and color-coded

---

[100] alewebsocial.com/TrelloPM

labels allow you to categorize activities for easy filtering of the information. To learn more, read "Using Trello to Manage Your Activities."[101]

The goal-setting step of the process is important. So, don't skip over it. Having a target to aim for shifts our focus and gives us the impetus we need to get up and do something. Otherwise, any book campaign you put together will have to limp along of its own accord without any real acknowledgement of its importance and without any means of determining its success. After all the time and effort you put into writing the book and researching things thus far, you don't want to have that happen, do you?

Here's where things start to get a bit tricky. There are two schools of thought regarding how bestseller campaigns should run. There are those individuals who like to amass a group of "JV partners" (or "joint venture

---

[101] alewebsocial.com/TrelloActivities

partners") and those who prefer to focus their time and attention on attracting just the right customer. We'll call this second group the "purists" just to be able to distinguish the two schools of thought.

I'll lay out the campaign proceedings for both, and you determine which one is best for you. You may find that you take bits and pieces from both methods for your attempt at bestseller status.

JV Partner Program

Creating a JV partner program leverages the networks of other individuals, which quickly and easily gives your book massive exposure. However, these programs have been offered so many times now that many people have become jaded about them. They may buy your book when it's something they wouldn't otherwise buy, simply to get the free bonuses. Yet, with time, they never actually get around to using the bonuses either. So, they feel gypped. The overall feeling is a negative one that could have a significant backlash for you or your book.

Therefore, if you're going to consider setting up a JV partner program for your book sale, make sure that the prospective partners you approach are *really* relevant to your readers, and that the bonuses they offer are of a standard you can support.

If you decide this approach is the right one for you, here's what you're going to do next.

Create a list of all affiliates, bloggers, fans, etc. that have expressed an interest in supporting your book. Ask if they would like to contribute relevant bonus products to your campaign effort.

Set up a simple webpage where these bonus products can be offered as incentives for buying your book on the date of the sale. The individuals who offer bonus products become your JV partners. To maximize the exposure for their own products, they are often willing to support you in increasing the exposure for yours.

Do some research to identify the names of marketers and individuals that have large mailing lists aimed at your target audience. Convince relevant list owners as to why their readers would welcome a marketing message about your book. For those that are interested, offer them the opportunity to become JV partners as well.

You can also do additional internet research to find reports and other free products of interest to your target audience. Request permission from the owners of those products to add them to your campaign bonuses.

Write a series of marketing and sales messages that your JV partners can share with their lists and networks. Put them together in a swipe file to make it easy for them to promote your book sale. Consider hiring a copywriter just to make sure you get these messages right.

Figure out what you're going to require to confirm a book purchase and provide the link to your bonus page. Sometimes, authors have buyers forward a copy of the sales receipt to a special e-mail address that is set up on an auto-responder. That way, once the receipt is received, the auto-responder immediately sends a note confirming receipt and providing access information to the buyer.

Alternatively, if your JV partners are willing to let you give their content away indefinitely, you can simply incorporate a link to the bonus materials into your actual book. That way, they have the information they need within the book itself.

The Purist Approach

Purists are more interested in finding prospective buyers that really have an interest in their book, not in any freebies that might be offered.

If this sounds more like you, here's what you're going to do. You'll be spending more of your time focused on ensuring that your book is properly categorized and tagged within Amazon so that it's easily found in searches.

You'll also want create a Listmania list in Amazon that matches your book with others that complement it well.

This will generate visibility for your book as prospective buyers look at any of the other books in your list.

You'll still reach out to any list owners with large lists that are aimed at your target audience to ask them if they'd be willing to include a marketing message about your book in their newsletter. But you won't be asking them for any bonus products.

You'll work with your existing network, seeking to grow it and nurturing new relationships, and ask them to help promote your book on its sale day.

While this approach is more labor-intensive, it lacks the potential for a backlash that the JV approach has and is more authentic.

Networking Meetings

Believe it or not, I sell copies of my books more regularly at networking meetings than anywhere else. I never go to a meeting without having at least a few books with me. It's a great visual when I give my 30-second elevator speech and can hold up one of my books as I tell people that I'm an award-winning, bestselling author, speaker and publisher, and that I help other authors and speakers get found online.

Invariably, people want to talk with me and often will buy a copy of my book while we speak. Which means, I made a point a long time ago of making sure that I had the means to process a credit card transaction right there and then. I had one too many awkward situations where someone wanted to buy a copy but one or the other of us didn't have the right change at the moment to make it happen.

I personally use the PayPal Here app[102] and reader and can process a payment in a matter of seconds, as well as send the buyer a receipt for their purchase. It demolishes the barrier to buying and ensures that I don't ever miss a sale again.

---

[102] alewebsocial.com/PayPalHere

Book Signings

Most authors will tell you that holding a book signing event is a waste of time and effort, and, for the most part, that's true. However, there are new spins on book signing events that *do* work much better than the traditional signing that takes place in your local bookstore.

Consider holding a book signing at an organization where your book is relevant. If your book is for entrepreneurs, find Meetup groups for entrepreneurs in your area and see if one would like to have you come speak a bit about your book and hold a book signing.

If you've written for a faith-based community, find churches in your area that might be interested in holding a special event.

You can often make the idea more appealing by finding another author who has books written for the same audience as yours and joining together to do some promotional activities.

In my home state of Connecticut, there's an organization of authors that holds book signing events together. It's called the American Authors and Publishers Guild[103] and they are working to expand beyond the Connecticut borders.

The Guild often has 20-30 authors signing their books at the same place, whether they share a target audience or not. Since people are often interested in more than one subject, many times readers will discover new books (and authors) they'd never hear of otherwise by attending one of these events.

Another Connecticut-based organization, the Connecticut Authors and Publishers Association[104] (CAPA), does something similar at The Big E, also known as the "New England State Fair," held just across the border in Massachusetts each September.

---

[103] alewebsocial.com/AAPG
[104] alewebsocial.com/CAPA

Part of membership in CAPA includes the opportunity to have your book sold in the Connecticut Bookstore at the fair and to hold a book signing there.

Press Releases

Did you know that press releases are still alive and well? PRWeb[105] is probably the largest and most visible press release site and they periodically offer you the opportunity to post a release for free, but it's always part of a trial offer. So, if you choose to use this service and it's not in the budget to pay for it, be judicious about how you decide to use it.

Instead, you may want to spend some time looking into alternative press release resources. Although it's a bit old, Mashable put together a list of 20+ Free Press

---

[105] alewebsocial.com/PRWeb

Release Distribution Sites[106] that still contains useful information describing the various sites available and how they differ. So, if you anticipate sending out more than one or two press releases, pick one of these sites to work with, rather than learning PRWeb, and then having to learn a second site when the budget runs dry.

There is also a site called Pressit,[107] which is a free, user-friendly Social Media News Release (SMNR) service. It allows you to create and publish a SMNR on the site using pre-selected categories. The release is then available via RSS feeds that can be pulled into any online reader. When published, your SMNR will be accessible to relevant audiences, including bloggers, social networks and other online communities. It can also be shared via social networks such as Facebook and Twitter or via an email link to your colleagues or press contacts.

---

[106] alewebsocial.com/PRSites
[107] alewebsocial.com/Pressit

Don't hesitate to reach out to your local media as well. You can find relevant contacts for your state at USNPL,[108] including newspaper, radio and TV outlets, location addresses, social media feeds, local libraries and museums, etc. While it's not a very attractive site, the amount of information you can find there is incredible. Use it to build your targeted recipient list for your press release, and start sending!

The whole point of a press release or a social media news release is to announce something that's noteworthy about you and your book. Don't hesitate to toot your own horn sometimes. It's in the best interest of your book, after all! And if bloggers, reporters and other news outlets aren't aware of what's going on with you and your book, they can't write about you!

Just keep in mind that many press releases go without ever being picked up. So, while this is an important

---

[108] alewebsocial.com/USNPL

activity to do, never prioritize it higher than those activities you're doing where you see results.

E-mail

You have to be very careful about what you send to people in your contact list. Unless they've specifically signed up to be on your mailing list, you run the risk of running afoul of government rules against SPAM. So, be aware of what the rules[109] are and do what you need to do to remain in compliance with them.

Yet there is a benefit to creating an e-mail list. When you create one properly, these individuals have "opted in" to hear from you periodically. Do *not* abuse that privilege. Consider what it is that they'd like to hear from you about and limit your communications to those things. And never, ever share that list with anyone else.

---

[109] alewebsocial.com/CanSpam

Additionally, make sure you update your e-mail signature to include information regarding the book, and links to your online presence. A tool that works well with web-based mail clients is called WiseStamp.[110] I use it all the time because it allows me to define my signature and include my social profiles in a clean and easy way. I can also maintain multiple signatures and switch between them at will. They do have an Outlook extension as well, but it's harder to implement and is only available to premium users.

Non-Bookstore Buyers

Most authors strive for the achievement of seeing their book on a bookstore shelf, and I'll admit, it feels great when it happens! But what most authors don't realize is, the majority of sales don't take place in a bookstore. In fact, more sales take place at online

---

[110] alewebsocial.com/WiseStamp

retailers and "Lemonade Lucy Stands," as a friend of mine calls them, than at brick-and-mortar bookstores.

However, that's not the only way to sell your book. And in fact, trying to compete for bookstore shelf space with the thousands of other titles published each year is almost a waste of your precious time and resources.

Instead, consider focusing some of your marketing efforts on non-bookstore buyers.

There are ways to sell large quantities of non-returnable books that only require the right connections, a modest budget, and a little ingenuity. That's where a service like The Promotional Bookstore[111] comes in. Founded by Brian Jud from Book Marketing Works,[112] The Promotional Bookstore is a catalogue that goes out to 65,000 sales professionals who already have the established contacts to sell your book as a promotional

---

[111] alewebsocial.com/PromoBookstore
[112] alewebsocial.com/BookMarketingWorks

item to corporations, churches, nonprofits and other large non-bookstore organizations.

As of the time of this writing, you can list your book in The Promotional Bookstore for as little as $250 for the lifetime of your title, making it available as a resource to a large number of buyers looking for promotional products. And while it can take as long as a year or more before an order for your book is placed, it is a solid investment to make in the success of your book because the order quantity is often large.

Brian Jud, who founded CAPA, an organization mentioned earlier in this book, is also the Executive Director of the Association of Publishers for Special Sales[113] (APSS). This organization provides guidance and expertise to its members based on the evolving nature of the book-publishing industry. It leverages opportunities ignored by most publishers to market great books to non-

---

[113] alewebsocial.com/APSS

bookstore buyers, including opportunities to find government buyers, create cross-selling opportunities, and more.

This organization is another great resource for authors because of all of the educational materials, webinars, etc. that it provides to its members who are trying to educate themselves on establishing special sales markets for their titles.

If you want to do more of the legwork yourself, you can also make use of sources like WEDDLE's Directory,[114] which is a database of associations, categorized by industry. With a little creative thinking you can find all sorts of opportunities to make your book relevant to their members. Start by selecting a category that your ideal reader might be in. Identify an association within that category to research.

---

[114] alewebsocial.com/Weddles

If it has a bookstore on its site, contact the bookstore manager to see how to list your title there.

You can also go to the membership chair for the association and propose that they offer a copy of your book to every member as part of an Early Bird membership renewal drive. For example, those who renew before the deadline get a one-time use download code for a digital copy of your book.

You can also go to the newsletter editor and offer excerpts of your book as content for the newsletter. You may even be able to negotiate ad space in the newsletter in exchange for the content. If you do though, consider a strategy where you post an independent review of your book the first month, an excerpt the second month, and run the ad in the third month. Let the readers become familiar with you and create that hunger to have more.

You can also go to the meeting chair and offer to speak. Help them see why your book would be a great way to thank their attendees for registering for the conference. Once again, this may be offered as an Early Bird special to get the registrations coming in.

This next strategy works with both nonprofit organizations and with associations, and it's simply this. Have them purchase copies of your book at a discounted price that they can then use as a fundraiser by charging list price for the book.

If you do decide to pursue associations though, don't spend your time pursuing the regional level chapters. It'll be way too time-consuming. Instead, start at the national level. Information will trickle down to the regions from there.

Another non-bookstore buyer who happens to purchase a lot of books each year is the U.S. government! You can visit the FedBizOpps website[115] to identify the right people to approach with your sales idea. You can also go to individual military exchanges (for example, the

---

[115] alewebsocial.com/FedBizOpps

Navy Exchange[116] and the Army & Air Force Exchange Service[117]) and find out who the buyer is for those sites to see if you can interest them in your title.

So, what happens if you're a self-publisher working with a Print-on-Demand source, like CreateSpace, and you suddenly get an order for 10,000 printed copies of your book? There are resources out there that can help you. My publishing imprint, Emerald Lake Books,[118] has the connections necessary to have your title printed with an offset printer and shipped to the buyer directly for you. So, not to worry!

If that same large quantity was ordered for eBooks instead, you could use a service to create one-time use, customized download cards (called "DropCards"[119]) that your buyer can distribute as they choose. You can either

---

[116] alewebsocial.com/Navy

[117] alewebsocial.com/ArmyAirForce

[118] alewebsocial.com/ELB

[119] alewebsocial.com/DropCards. Use the coupon code "AlewebSocial" to receive a 10% discount on your next order.

have your graphic designer (or ours!) use one of their templates to create a card for you or you can use their in-house services to have them design one instead. Once the cards are printed, they can be shipped directly to your buyer for immediate use.

Crowdsourcing

If you've read this far into *The Plan*, I'm sure by now you've realized that marketing and promoting a book takes a lot of time and effort. And some of the things I recommend here may be better handled by a professional.

The problem is: not everyone who writes has a budget to work with.

Sure, if your book is being published by a traditional publisher, you may have an advance to work with. But for most self-publishers, the marketing budget is practically non-existent.

Hopefully, there are enough ideas in this book to help you get started in generating some revenue on your own. I highly recommend sinking it right back into making your book a success. You've worked hard and deserve it!

But there is another means of pulling together a budget that's becoming more popular all the time. It's called "crowdsourcing" or "crowdfunding."

You may be familiar already with sites like Kickstarter and IndieGogo, where people pitch a project they're working on or a product they want to create and interested people back the project by investing in it. A few dollars invested by hundreds or even thousands of people goes a long way, without straining anyone's wallet.

Each crowdfunding site has its own requirements about what projects it will accept, and what their acceptance criteria are. They also offer different campaign models with varying fee schedules. So be sure to dig into all of the details about the campaign process before deciding which site to use and how to define your campaign.

It's important to note too that there's a science behind the wording that's used in your campaign and the psychological impact it has on the potential donor. One of the best people I've met at explaining all that is Jason W. Nast. If you ever have the chance to discuss it with him, by all means, do! And if you have a spare hour and fifteen minutes, you may want to check out his webinar on Crowdfunding for Information Products.[120] (Keep in mind, a book is an information product. But so is an audiobook, a DVD, a webinar, etc. The material that Jason presents in this webinar is suitable for all of them.)

He's the one who taught me that the first 24 to 48 hours of your campaign are the most critical. It doesn't matter if the campaign is set to run for 2 weeks, a month

---

[120] alewebsocial.com/CrowdfundingWebinar

or even 6 weeks. What happens in those first few hours will dictate how the rest of the campaign goes. Why?

Because the crowdsourcing sites look to see which campaigns have the marketing know-how to get a jumpstart right out of the gate. And when they find one, they back it. If your campaign catches their eye, they will promote it to their mailing list, give it front page placement, and create more visibility for it than you could ever do on your own.

So, it's not just a matter of knowing how to put the campaign together and what verbiage to use to convert potential donors into paying customers, it's also about knowing how you're going to get the word out, what publicity to put in place, and how to coordinate the whole thing so that the timing all falls into place.

It's also about knowing what to ask for. You see, what the crowdsourcing site is looking for is, they want to see you reach at least half of your goal in that first day or two. That's how they know whether your campaign is a winner or not.

You may think that it makes the most sense to put together a budget that outlines all of the costs you could ever possibly have for marketing and promoting your book. But actually, the opposite is true. Much like knowing your target audience for a marketing campaign, you have to know your target project for a crowdsourcing campaign. Be precise and keep the costs low. Jason told me a year ago that campaigns that are looking to raise less than $5K are something like 83% likely to be fulfilled. Whereas, campaigns seeking $5K or more are only 10% likely to be fulfilled.

Part of that is because it's easier to reach 50% of $4500 in the first 24 hours than it is to reach $25K, but the other part is because people are more likely to contribute if they feel like your goal is attainable. If they think it's outrageous, they're less likely to "throw their money away."

So, it's better to have multiple smaller projects than to have one large over-arching project. Keep in mind, if you exceed your goal, you get everything that was donated. It's much better to set a lower goal and exceed it than to set a higher one and not reach it, especially because some campaigns only receive funding if the goal is met or they charge a higher fee if you don't meet your goal.

Setting a goal that you can meet will keep costs down and assure that you receive what's been donated. (Just in case you're wondering, if you run a campaign where the goal is not met, and it's one that you only receive funding when the goal is met, your contributors aren't charged. The money they pledged to the campaign is never drawn from their accounts.)

While Kickstarter and IndieGogo are fairly well-known crowdsourcing sites, there is also a newer one out there that caters specifically to the literary world. It's called Pubslush.[121] Founded by mother and daughter entrepreneurs, Hellen and Amanda Barbara, who wanted to create a more democratic publishing process after learning about the struggles of authors like J.K. Rowling, whose bestselling series was rejected by the 12 publishers to which it was initially sent. They felt that too many great authors have been dismissed to the infamous "slush pile." So, the name of their site is derived from their mission to give authors the opportunity to get out of the slush pile, prove their talent and market viability, and successfully publish quality books.

Each campaign has its own page, regardless of what site you use, and you're able to send updates to your donors throughout the campaign. This can become a great way to collect pre-orders for your book as a self-publisher and build your mailing list, if you do it right, and continued reminders that the campaign is running

---

[121] alewebsocial.com/Pubslush

reminds your existing contributors to share the information with their friends.

A final note about crowdfunding though. It's something many of us tend not to think about, but must be accounted for. When you run a crowdsourcing campaign and receive the donated funds, you have to account for applicable taxes. So, be sure to consult with your accountant or tax preparer in advance to understand the impact of a successful campaign on your finances.

Conclusion

There's a lot of content in this plan. That's because a book launch, properly done, takes a lot of work! But pace yourself. Choose those things that resonate with you most and tackle those first. Marketing your book is an ongoing process, not a one-time venture.

You may find there are things here that you never get around to doing. That's okay. This simply gives you a picture of the scope of a book launch campaign and what can be done with it.

There is one final thing you may want to know now that you've reached the end of this plan, and hopefully you've implemented a bunch of the recommendations in it. The work you've done here? It's one of the things that acquiring editors for major media outlets look for when they review an author's proposal. Alan Rinzler mentions in his blog, The Book Deal:[122]

> ...one of the first things I look for in an author's proposal is the "platform", that is, the writer's reputation and public visibility – and the ability, willingness, and experience to promote themselves in the marketplace.
>
> What we publishers all hope for when opening a proposal from a literary agent is not just a great idea for a book and a promising ability to write, but an aspiring author's track record in book sales, appearances on radio and television, respect in the professional community for teaching, research, and scholarship, as well as financial success in the field and anything else that has put the author's name in public and produced a long list of entries on Google.
>
> The bigger the platform, the higher the book advance.

---

[122] alewebsocial.com/BookDeal

You can read the rest of his post on how to "Build your author platform: 10 tips from a pro."[123] But the message is clear. Building visibility for yourself and your book only serves to put you in a better position when you're ready to publish your next one!

If you have questions about anything in this book or if you're interested in having me come speak with your company or group about book marketing, feel free to contact us here at Aleweb Social Marketing.[124] We'd be happy to answer what we can. In the meantime, have fun!

**Aleweb Social Marketing
is committed to
your book marketing success!**

*Connect with us online, and let us know
which tip you found most valuable
for marketing your book
using the hashtag #1KBooks!*

---

[123] alewebsocial.com/10Tips
[124] alewebsocial.com/contact

The book is sponsored by:

Aleweb Social Marketing
alewebsocial.com

Tara R. Alemany
tararalemany.com

The Bite-Sized Marketer
bitesizedmarketer.com

Emerald Lake Books
emeraldlakebooks

Gerber Studio
gerberstudio.com

• • •

If you like what you've read here
and want a free 30-minute coaching session
with Tara, sign up for more information at
alewebsocial.com/authors.

• • •

Please leave us a review on Amazon[125]
if you enjoyed this book.
It helps to know whether or not
it has been valuable to you.

---

[125] alewebsocial.com/ThePlanAmazon

About the Author

Tara R. Alemany is an award-winning, bestselling and nationally known inspirational author, speaker, social marketing consultant and publisher.

She has authored two books, and co-authored or contributed to three others. Her latest book, *The Best is Yet to Come*,[126] was released in November 2013, and shares the lessons learned while overcoming the unexpected death of her fiancé in October 2011.

Tara speaks frequently on social media, publishing and inspirational topics, and is the creator and host of The Survivors Summit (renamed to "Inspiring Hope" in

---

[126] alewebsocial.com/BIYTC

2014[127]), a virtual inspirational conference held in November, where she brings together powerful speakers with amazing stories of overcoming adversity who created lives of power, passion and purpose as a result.

Tara is the owner and founder of Aleweb Social Marketing,[128] a consulting company that helps authors, speakers and entrepreneurs use their talents to grow their businesses by strategically positioning themselves online, on-stage and on-the-shelf.

Aleweb offers services ranging from book preparation (editing, formatting and publishing through its Emerald Lake Books[129] imprint) through to website design and social profile development, and the training and strategies required to reach your target market with your unique message.

---

[127] alewebsocial.com/Hope
[128] alewebsocial.com
[129] alewebsocial.com/ELB

She is also the creator of The Bite-Sized Marketer,[130] a video tutorial subscription service that guides you through the process of marketing yourself online, one bite at a time.

Tara's thoughts and insights have also been included in articles on Carol Roth's Business Unplugged, Marketing Sherpa and Bank of America's Small Business brief, and her content has been reprinted in SOLDLab magazine, Business2Community and AllTop.

Tara also facilitates a mastermind group[131] that helps serious business people get serious business results. If you want to be considered for an upcoming group and learn directly from Tara how to achieve your goals, be sure to check it out.

In addition to consulting, writing and speaking, Tara serves on the Boards of Directors for a Christian writers'

---

[130] alewebsocial.com/BSM
[131] alewebsocial.com/Mastermind

critique group and is Chaplain of that same group. In her spare time, she is a novice wine maker, a martial artist, a juggler, Mom to 2 teenagers (one of each), step-Mom to 2 dogs (one of each) and is owned by a black cat.